VOICES OF WINCHESTER
WORLD WAR II
VETERANS

··

ADRIAN J. O'CONNOR

THE
History
PRESS

Published by The History Press
Charleston, SC
www.historypress.com

Front cover, top left: courtesy of the family of U.S. Senator Harry F. Byrd Jr.; *top center*: courtesy of the Stewart Bell Jr. Archives, Winchester, Virginia; *top right*: courtesy of the Stewart Bell Jr. Archives, Winchester, Virginia; *bottom*: courtesy of the Stewart Bell Jr. Archives, Winchester, Virginia.
Back cover: courtesy of the Stewart Bell Jr. Archives, Winchester, Virginia.

First published 2023

Manufactured in the United States

ISBN 9781467151290

Library of Congress Control Number: 2022949639

Notice: The information in this book is true and complete to the best of our knowledge. It is offered without guarantee on the part of the author or The History Press. The author and The History Press disclaim all liability in connection with the use of this book.

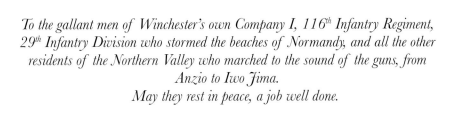

To the gallant men of Winchester's own Company I, 116th Infantry Regiment, 29th Infantry Division who stormed the beaches of Normandy, and all the other residents of the Northern Valley who marched to the sound of the guns, from Anzio to Iwo Jima.
May they rest in peace, a job well done.

CONTENTS

WE WALK IN THEIR FOOTSTEPS

When I was growing up in the late 1950s and early to mid-1960s, in addition to our usual seasonal rounds of pickup games and youth sports—Little League baseball, Pop Warner football and Biddie basketball—my friends and I played "army."

It was an odd and unique exercise. Our "equipment," as it were, was of World War II style, but what our toy guns and bazookas fired at was mostly invisible, conjured up by ten-year-old imaginations. Sometimes, we could cajole a rival neighborhood gang to be our "enemy," but that was rare. So we pursued Germans and Japanese of the mind.

What we did not realize was that the war was still fresh in the minds of our dads and moms and other adults. Our playtime military exercises were just twenty years or so removed from the real thing. And so, in a very real sense, we were imitating our fathers, even if we did not quite grasp the notion.

But then again, maybe we did. These veterans, after all, occupied the main-traveled roads of our lives. My dad was a vet, and so were three of his four brothers. My Uncle Jack gained some local acclaim as a logistician almost at the elbow of General Omar Bradley.

My closest childhood buddy's father, to cite another example, was either a navigator or a bombardier—I can never remember which—in the Pacific air wars, and I vividly recall the weekend when he and one of his fellow aviators reconstructed the airstrip at Kwajalein on a huge piece of canvas in his garage.

Likewise, one of my father's fellow Little League coaches was a sturdy, square-built Marine who had witnessed the horrors of Iwo Jima. And though his experiences may have been exceptional, he was hardly an exception around our New Jersey town. He was rather the norm. The "greatest generation" walked among us long before it was considered "great." We were blessed to have lived in their presence day after day.

Blessed, too, was to have met, later in life, the men whose stories fill the pages of this book. It was like reuniting with the men I had known so well almost a half century earlier. And in these instances, the stories left untold in my childhood—the memories of war were too vivid and fresh back then—came tumbling from the mouths of veterans eager at last to inform later generations what had happened on Omaha Beach, or at Anzio, or in the skies over Ploesti, or in the deepest part of "The Bulge" or, much like my dad's friend, in the hellfires of Iwo Jima.

These newer generations need such knowledge, as do all Americans, if only to bring back the slightest sense of realism to those beloved neighborhood games—that is, if kids still do, in fact, play "army."

Only in these ways—through recordation on the pages of history, popular as well as academic, and wholesome, emblematic play in backyards, farm fields and wooded demesnes all across this land—will the "greatness" of that generation remain in full bloom.

I can only hope this small volume contributes to such necessary reminiscence. I treasured every moment spent with these "ordinary" men who did "extraordinary" things, to paraphrase the famous words of Admiral Chester Nimitz, whether decades ago in the flower of their youth or in their vintage recalling their stirring stories for posterity.

—Adrian J. O'Connor
September 6, 2021

ACKNOWLEDGEMENTS

All literary endeavors, even books as modest as the one you are about to read, are hardly solitary pursuits. Authors, if they're lucky, always have a little help from their friends.

I know I did.

For example, if I were not blessed with the help of my research assistant, Reed Davis, this effort would have died aborning. Even though I spent four decades in the newspaper business, I remain a blank slate in a technical sense. Maybe a know-nothing is more accurate.

Well, Reed, a graduate student at Shenandoah University in Winchester, is a know-*something*. Needless to say, if I didn't have him navigating the electronic maze, I would have just a mess of articles and photos, not a book. Thanks, Reed, for all of your guidance.

I am thankful as well for the patience of Kate Jenkins, my editor at The History Press / Arcadia Press, who somehow shepherded me through the intricacies of the publisher's Rules for Authors.

Over the years, my editors at the *Winchester Star*, for which these articles were originally written, put up with my "long-form" tendencies in pretty much every feature I wrote. Let me say that when cutting was done, it was done judiciously.

It's been forever said—and accurately so—that behind every man there's a good and/or great woman. Both adjectives apply in the person of Toni O'Connor. She is my inspiration.

Finally, I could not let this page pass without thanking the many veterans who gladly, or so it seemed, suffered a writer's interminable questioning. Many vets opt to remain mum about their oft-searing wartime experiences. These men did not. How could I express my thanks other than to recognize and adhere to the integrity and dignity of their stories?

I hope I did so. Enjoy.

A QUIET SUNDAY IN 1941

T hough levity was hardly a prescription for the moment, former U.S. senator Harry F. Byrd Jr. can chuckle today at his initial reaction to the news that Japanese warplanes had attacked the U.S. Pacific Fleet at Pearl Harbor.

Byrd, then the editor and general manager of the *Winchester Evening Star*, was enjoying a relaxed Sunday lunch with family members on December 7, 1941—sixty years ago today—when the Associated Press phoned with the news at about 2:00 p.m.

The AP representative wanted to know if the newspaper planned to publish an extra edition about the attack. Byrd initially said no; he didn't think the newspaper would publish any sort of "special."

"It was so unbelievable what they said the Japanese had done," Byrd said this week from his office at the *Star*. So I said, 'No.'

"I got back to the table and we started discussing the attack, and then I realized what I had said. I called the AP right back and said, 'Of course, we want to publish an extra.'"

After informing the AP of his decision, Byrd immediately called Ralph Fansler, the newspaper's business manager, and requested that he assemble the staff. He also phoned his family's other newspaper, the *Daily News-Record* in Harrisonburg, and relayed his intent to publish an extra edition about the attack.

As Byrd recollected, the type for the special section was set in Winchester and taken to Harrisonburg by car. The extra, dated December 8, hit the streets early that morning.

Byrd was hardly alone in his profession of "unbelievability." One must remember that, although World War II was raging in Europe and the United States was supporting the war effort through Lend-Lease, the attack on Pearl Harbor caught almost everyone off-guard.

December 7, 1941, was just another Sunday in America, roughly two weeks before Christmas. Many folks had returned from church services and were, like Byrd, sitting down to dinner or lunch when the reports came crackling over the radio.

In fact, Sydney Willey of Woodland Avenue in Winchester was listening to a Dixieland show from New Orleans—Dinah Shore was the featured vocalist—when the program

Lieutenant Commander (and future U.S. Senator) Harry F. Byrd Jr. in naval khakis. *Courtesy of the Stewart Bell Jr. Archives, Winchester, Virginia.*

was interrupted. "I thought, 'Why are they interrupting Dinah Shore to announce this?'," Willey recalled. "We didn't know where this place Pearl Harbor was. We sure learned all about it really quick, though."

Like Willey, most people were simply following the even tenor of their ways that Sunday. For example, Ernie Brindle, a Standard Oil retiree now living in Winchester, was a freshman at Shippensburg State College (now University) in 1941. He was home for the weekend in Gettysburg, Pennsylvania, when he heard the news. He returned to college the same day.

Lewis Ebert of Fox Drive in Winchester was ten years old when the Japanese struck Pearl Harbor. He especially recalled gathering around the family radio and listening to President Franklin D. Roosevelt's impassioned and stirring speech following the attack. "He was a great orator," said Ebert, later a longtime employee of the *Star*.

Ebert's four older brothers, all Handley High School grads, would serve in the armed forces. John, the oldest, was with the U.S. Army Air Corps in the China-Burma-India theater of conflict. Lee was a combat engineer in Europe.

Charles, a member of the fabled 8th Air Force, participated in thirty-five combat missions as a gunner. Douglas was in Korea, preparing for the proposed invasion of Japan, when the war ended. Ebert himself is a veteran of the Korean War.

For some, the attack on Pearl Harbor hit a bit closer to home. Ann Murphy Bullis, who has lived in the Brookneil community in Frederick

Harry F. Byrd Jr. in action shot. *Courtesy of the family of U.S. Senator Harry F. Byrd Jr.*

County for the past six years, was four years old in 1941. She and her family were worshipping at the Church of the Pilgrims in downtown Washington when her father, Captain John Vernon Murphy, was summoned to Navy headquarters. "Even then, I knew it was serious," Bullis said, "but we had so much family around us. I was never made to feel like we were in danger."

Horses gambol on present-day Omaha Beach, Normandy, France. *Courtesy of the O'Connor family.*

John Murphy served as head of naval communications, retiring with the rank of commodore.

With the staff working feverishly on the next day's editions, Harry F. Byrd Jr. wrote the editorial that would appear on the front page of the "extra."

His words were clear, concise, to the point:

"The developments of the past twelve hours are almost unbelievable. The madness of Japan is staggering. 'Without provocation, a foreign power has attacked United States naval bases, the harbors of a nation at peace.' 'This attack has been followed by a Japanese declaration of war against the United States.'

"'Japan will be answered in kind.' 'Congress will declare war immediately.' 'There is no alternative.'

"'Yesterday, the people of the United States were peace-loving, peaceful.' 'Today, we are no less peace-loving, only less peaceful.'

"'Yesterday, our people were sharply divided, wholly disunited.' 'Today we are as one.'

"'Every resource of this resourceful nation—of these united people—will be used to annihilate our enemy.'"

It would take the better part of four years for this aim to be achieved.

On December 7, 1941, the long haul toward victory had already begun. America, once again, was at war.

1

D-DAY

D-Day was the pivot point of the 20th century. It was the day on which it was decided whether the world was going to be Nazi or was going to be democratic.
—Historian Stephen Ambrose

OMAHA BEACH

VIERVILLE-SUR-MER, France—It was 6:45 a.m. The sun, rising over the Bay of the Seine, had just emerged from behind a billowing cumulus cloud. As I reached the beach at Les Moulins last Tuesday, I was alone—and it was perfect.

It was so unlike that morning sixty-three years and two months ago to the hour when the feet of local boys—with names like Clowe and Clevenger, Orndorff and Wohlford—touched that same stretch of sand. That day was dull and overcast. They were cold. Many were scared. Even more were seasick. And waiting for them on the bluffs above the beach were the might and manpower of Nazi Germany.

For them, the boys of Winchester's Company I, it was far from perfect. Rather, it was more like a cloudy picture of chaos, of hell on earth.

Less than an hour before, their comrades in other companies of the 116th Regiment, 29th Infantry Division, had walked into the teeth of deadly German fire, so many never to return. Some of our boys—Tech Sergeant John Sheppard Wohlford, for one—met this same fate.

But because they did, and because so many more fought on and breached Adolf Hitler's allegedly impregnable Atlantic Wall that "longest day," I could walk that same beach, forever to be known as Omaha, with hardly a care. I could stride in peace across those sectors of sand that once bore the code names Dog Red, Dog White and Dog Green.

Sixty-three years later, I saw nothing of the carnage. But what I did see was illuminating—seashells, the remains of play forts built the previous day, a heart etched in the sand symbolizing young love.

Later, I would pass youngsters walking their dog, and a jogger or two. And when my wife, Toni, and I returned later that morning, we witnessed, for us, a rare and beautiful sight—two ponies, their hooves splashing in the surf, pulling their respective buggies, or traps.

Yes, a war once took place on that beach, one seared in our collective memory, and thankfully so, for we must never forget.

But on a sunny French morning, all was calm and serene, as well it should be. Yes, illustrated plaques dot the shoreline describing what transpired that June day years ago, but they're hardly obtrusive. Omaha Beach is a place of subdued, understated remembrance—and for this we should give those perennially grateful residents of Normandy their just due.

At Vierville, overlooking Dog Green, are the monuments—but again, nothing ostentatious, just simple reminders that the 29th Division came ashore there and that the Army Rangers, who had conquered the steep cliffs of Pointe du Hoc just a short ride away, had also led the way through the heavily defended Vierville draw. And, finally, the memorial to the citizen-soldiers, erected by the U.S. National Guard, sits atop what looks to be the remains of a German bunker at the mouth of that once-fearful draw.

So long ago, I thought, but not so far away, as I stood there, taking one long, last look at a place I had read reams about but never thought I would see.

Here, unvarnished heroism and simple love for one's fellow soldier made their stand one grim day and beat the odds arrayed against them. Here, the pride of Virginia, the young men from the farms, villages and small towns of the Old Dominion who composed the gallant 116th, struck a telling blow for civilization.

As I turned and headed back toward Les Moulins and my car, I noticed another sign. It yielded no further details of the deadly transactions of that fateful morning but rather provided safety instructions for swimmers enjoying the sunny delights of Omaha Beach.

That, in itself, is a fitting and wonderful tribute to the valiant Americans who secured those sands, for freedom's sake, one hellish June day in 1944.

Dead of Night:
Carroll Palmer Takes Flight

One thing we knew, sometime we'd have to go to Europe.
We flew day and night to prepare for this. But we didn't know
it was D-Day until it was very close.
—Carroll W. Palmer

Ever since that summer day in the 1930s when a daredevil barnstorming pilot buzzed the annual Adams County (Ohio) reunion in his biplane, Carroll W. Palmer knew he wanted to fly.

"It was so exciting," says Palmer, eighty-nine, seated at the dining-room table in his comfortable home off Apple Valley Road south of Winchester. The retired Shepherd University education professor quickly added, "It just set me on fire."

Little did Palmer realize that the flicker of youthful dreams would turn into blazing reality, literally and figuratively, in the fires of war.

Sixty-five years ago today—June 5, 1944—he was just one of many U.S. Army Air Corps pilots pacing and pondering, waiting anxiously for the word and wondering whether stormy skies would clear so they could write their names on the pages of history.

Carroll Palmer was waiting for D-Day.

From Ohio to England

If his mother, Margie, had gotten her way, Palmer would never have been on that English airstrip nervously anticipating a flight across the Channel.

He thought he wanted to fly; she thought he didn't. Mother won the initial battle of wills. She and her husband, E. Ray, refused to sign Carroll's application for flight training. He, of course, was drafted anyway.

On Groundhog Day 1942, he left a first-year teacher's job at Fairfield High School in Leesburg, Ohio, for his induction at Fort Thomas, Kentucky. Eventually transferred to the artillery at Fort Jackson, South Carolina, Palmer never relinquished his "flyboy" ambitions. He convinced his younger sister Donnabel to send him those flight application papers still sitting at home in West Union, Ohio.

This time, Palmer made it, since the U.S. Air Corps, he says succinctly, "needed pilots." Or warm bodies.

He wanted to fly B-17s, the fabled Flying Fortress. The corps had other ideas. He was assigned B-24s, the cumbersome Liberator he describes as "a truck with wings."

Still, he and copilot "Buddy" Paine were the first pair in their class at Tennessee's Smyrna Army Air Base to solo in the B-24.

Then came a break, though a "bitter" Palmer was loath to admit it at the time. He and Paine, unable to obtain the requisite "instrument time" to graduate with their class, suffered elimination from B-24 training. They were sent to Bergstrom Army Air Base in Texas to "transition" to C-47s, the corps' bellwether twin-engine transports.

Palmer loved flying at Bergstrom, and he loved the C-47. "The 30 days in Bergstrom, I enjoyed flying there more than anywhere," he says. "And the C-47 was fun, from the minute I got in one until the minute I got out. I didn't know then how I really lucked out, but I did."

By the time he passed through Fort Benning, Georgia, and Grenada Army Air Base in Mississippi, where he got a full crew, Palmer had logged many hours dropping paratroopers and towing gliders.

When he reached Morrison Field in West Palm Beach, Florida, he knew he was in the "pipeline" for assignment overseas. But where? Pilots were told not to open their orders until seated in the cockpit. Palmer's papers indicated his destination was "the United Kingdom" via Brazil and Liberia.

The trip took twenty-two days. On March 30, 1944, he landed in Welford Park, County of Berkshire.

Flights and "Fireworks"

Training in Welford Park was not "that much different" than in the States for Palmer and his crew, assigned to the 78th Squadron, 435th Troop Carrier Group. But they did learn to fly at night without lights, a suggestion of sorties to come.

C-47 pilots prepared for two specific missions critical to the invasion of Hitler's Fortress Europe. They would either drop paratroopers, men of the elite 82nd and 101st Airborne Divisions, in the dead of night; or they would tow gliders full of troops and equipment. Palmer, pilot of a designated "replacement" crew, drew the latter straw.

General Dwight Eisenhower, the supreme allied commander, was at Welford Park on the night of June 5–6 when the sodden skies suddenly cleared and the first C-47s took off, bound for the coast of France.

Palmer suited up on the evening of June 6, D-Night. Darkness, he says, "was fast approaching" when his C-47 flew over the Cotentin Peninsula and reached the drop zone for the glider, just south of the village of Sainte-Mère-Église, twelve to fifteen miles inland from the landing beaches on the Normandy coast.

The sky suddenly lit up. Flak surrounded the plane. "It was the prettiest sight I ever saw, the tracers and explosions," Palmer recalls. "It was a real fireworks display. I never saw anything prettier—or more frightening."

With fighter planes providing "good protection" from above, Palmer took his C-47 to about one thousand feet and let the glider go. "They cut loose," he says. "We didn't see them go down. Two weeks later, we learned they got in OK."

Palmer then dropped "as low as we could go" and released the towline "on the Germans" and headed for home base.

From Pilot to Educator

Palmer's war experience hardly ended with D-Day. He and his crew also participated in the ill-fated airdrop over Holland—Operation Market Garden—in September 1944, memorialized in the Cornelius Ryan book (and film of the same name) *A Bridge Too Far*.

Later, he dropped "Jerry cans" (five-gallon containers of gasoline) to General George Patton and his thirsty tanks and also flew supplies to the beleaguered defenders of Bastogne in those desperate days around Christmas 1944 during the Battle of the Bulge.

"That was one of the worst times," he says of the unnerving Bastogne relief effort.

"It was snowing and raining, and we couldn't get anything to them at first. But they were our buddies. You felt bad that you couldn't do anything to help. But when the weather cleared, we went over."

Upon returning to the United States in early July 1945, Palmer called a young teacher he had dated "about a half-dozen times" while in flight training at Maxwell Field in Montgomery, Alabama.

Ruth Price agreed to meet him at his parents' new home in Seaman, Ohio. Two days later, they took a bus to Maysville, Kentucky, and got married. "They said it wouldn't last," Palmer says with a grin. "But here we are, sixty-four years later."

After running his parents' grocery store for a year, Palmer, with his bride at his side, commenced an extended educational odyssey that saw him obtain two advanced degrees, not to mention a number of jobs as both a teacher and school administrator.

Ruth taught at many stops along the way, and together they raised four children, Lea, Randy, Bob and Tom.

In 1969 came the last stop on this career journey, at Shepherd, where Palmer served as director of teacher education and taught courses in education and psychology. He retired in 1985.

Ten years later, precisely five decades removed from his final days in uniform, Palmer wrote an account of his military service, titled "My War Remembered." He dedicated it to Ruth.

Requiem for a Hometown Hero (Published September 1, 2007)

The infantry fights without promise of either reward or relief. Behind every river there's another hill—and behind that hill, another river. After weeks or months in the line only a wound can offer him the comfort of safety, shelter, and a bed. Those who are left to fight, fight on, evading death but knowing that with each day of evasion they have exhausted one more chance for survival. Sooner or later, unless victory comes, this chase must end on the litter or in the grave.
—General Omar Bradley

He rests eternally in Plot I, Row 5, Grave 19.

Recognition of his sacrifice is no different than for any other on this immaculate plateau of endless white crosses, save for one thing: His is a row interrupted by a breakage of trees and shrubbery.

And so Army Technical Sergeant John Sheppard Wohlford (Serial No. 20365269)—or Sheppard J. Wohlford, as the cross states in error—can forever claim the comforts of shade and protection from the elements, an accommodation sorely lacking when he stormed the beach directly below some sixty-three years ago.

In this, he is hardly alone. Many of his comrades in perpetual repose arrived in France as he did, aboard floating matchboxes, and died as he did, in the hellfires of that beach, now serene and known, ironically, as Omaha. Others made it to the bluffs, only to perish inland during the

John Sheppard "Shep" Wohlford. *Courtesy of the Stewart Bell Jr. Archives, Winchester, Virginia.*

triumphant drive toward Paris in that summer of 1944, in Norman towns such as Carentan, Avranches and St. Lo.

There are 9,386 crosses in all, some bearing no name. "Shep" Wohlford of Bartonsville and Winchester—and Company I, 116th Regiment, 29th Infantry Division—does not want for company.

But this windswept yet meticulously manicured tabletop in Normandy holds but his physical remains. The home fires of memory continue to burn across the sea in Connecticut, where his niece Rhoda Pigeon, daughter of his late sister Betty Wohlford Settle, lives. Or in Winchester, where Betty's other daughter, Liza Orndorff, resides with her husband, David, and their daughters, Katie and Emma.

And on South Stewart Street in Winchester, just a short walk from where Shep left home and hearth on Wolfe Street when his National Guard unit went on active duty in the winter of 1941, dwells his namesake, former city councilman John S. "Shep" Campbell.

No, Shep Wohlford is not forgotten, yet his is a story—and that of Company I as well—that is aching to be told.

He was a hard worker, unassuming, a nice guy.
Everyone liked him—and Mom thought the world of him.
—John S. "Shep" Campbell

Shep Wohlford—or John Sheppard Wohlford, as the conscientiously kept Campbell family Bible clearly notes—did not hail from the Northern Valley.

Rather, he and his three siblings—two girls and a boy—from the union of John S. and Mae Wohlford were born and largely came of age in Southwest Virginia, in the Bland County community of Mechanicsburg. Dwight, who came in 1912, was the oldest, followed by Marguerite (1915), Shep (born on August 17, 1917) and Betty (1919).

In a real sense, the Depression brought the family to Frederick County. The elder John, a circuit-riding doctor for the Consolidated Coal Company and a farmer to boot, had taken the advice of a brother and invested heavily in the manganese industry. The Depression hit, and the Wohlfords, says nephew Shep Campbell, "lost everything."

And so, in the dark economic days of the early 1930s, John Wohlford packed up family and belongings and moved north to the Shenandoah Valley, where, Campbell adds, "he always wanted to live" anyway.

The Wohlfords landed in Bartonsville, farm country just north of Stephens City, making their home on the Valley Pike in an eighteenth-century dwelling built by pioneering settler Joist Hite as a wedding present for his daughter. But John's stay in the valley he so desired proved to be short-lived. He died in 1934.

Though a county kid, Shep attended Handley High School in Winchester, where he played on the basketball team. He graduated in 1937, a well-liked member of a class that also included future Winchester mayor (and Company I combat leader) Mifflin B. Clowe and future construction magnate Ralph Shockey, as well as postwar local businessmen Harry Stewart and L. Marshall Boyd.

After graduation, Shep worked at the A&P grocery and, more tellingly, enlisted in Winchester's National Guard unit, Company I of the 116th, whose service lineage dates to the Augusta County Regiment, formed in 1742. The 116th—whose record takes a back seat to no one, says former 7th District congressman and Secretary of the Army John O. Marsh Jr., himself a former member—boasts battle streamers from almost every major American war.

From the French and Indian and Revolutionary conflicts through the Civil War (in which it was a vital part of the famed "Stonewall Brigade") and then in World War I, the men of the 116th distinguished themselves on fields of strife. But never more so than in World War II.

Still, when Shep signed on, America was still mired in the Depression and rumors of war were but a distant cry. He rose to the rank of platoon sergeant (in Company I's 1st Platoon) and frequently crossed paths with Charles Lillis, a weapons sergeant.

Lillis, a spry nonagenarian who still regularly ushers at the 7:30 a.m. Sunday Mass at Sacred Heart of Jesus Roman Catholic Church in Winchester, says he knew Shep well and liked him. "But then," he quickly adds, "everyone did. He was just a fine soldier."

With war looming in the winter of early 1941, the 116th, as a unit—and Shep with it—was inducted into federal service and assigned to the 29th ("Blue and Gray") Infantry Division. Composing the 29th were the 116th and two regiments from Maryland, the 115th and the 175th.

Following its induction at Staunton, the 116th was based at Maryland's Fort Meade. In the wake of Pearl Harbor, war preparations naturally intensified, and the regiment, nicknamed the "Stonewallers," moved from training ground to training ground—from Virginia's Fort A.P. Hill to North Carolina's Fort Bragg to Florida's Camp Blanding and, finally, to New Jersey's Camp Kilmer.

By then, Shep's family had moved from its Bartonsville farm to an apartment at Wolfe and Stewart Streets in Winchester. The relocation made sense. With gas rationing instituted and men leaving the Northern Valley for war in droves, the farm was more luxury than working operation, far too expensive to keep going. What's more, the Wohlford women had found

Charles Lillis. *Courtesy of the Stewart Bell Jr. Archives, Winchester, Virginia.*

work in town—Marguerite (by then married to Carl Campbell), for example, at the *Winchester Star.*

For Shep and his comrades, the transfer to Camp Kilmer predicated a longer trip to follow. After but a week's stay in New Jersey, the 29th, on September 27, 1942, boarded the luxury liner *Queen Mary*, quickly converted to a troop transport, and sailed from the Port of New York. Destination: England.

For the better part of a year, the 29th was the lone American division billeted on that "scepter'd isle." But, come the fall of 1943, America's might, in the form of men and material, began arriving by the boatload. Plans were well underway for an invasion of Hitler's "Festung Europa," or "Fortress Europe."

But where would that invasion take place? The Germans were guessing the Pas-de-Calais, the point on the French coast closest to England. But the site selected for intensive war games training suggested another invasion locale entirely.

In late December 1943 and early January 1944, Shep, the 116th and the rest of the 29th ventured to the south coast of England, to the beaches of Slapton Sands, for a final—and most rigorous—invasion rehearsal. Little did they know it at the time, but the terrain at Slapton Sands closely resembled that of the Normandy coast.

In May 1944, Shep wrote what proved to be his last letter home. He was still in England. By then, the 116th had been temporarily attached to the 1st Infantry Division, the "Big Red One." Something was clearly up. The long-anticipated invasion was imminent. But where would it take place—and when?

Omaha Beach became a symbol for all the horror that such seaborne operations entailed. Breaching Hitler's infamous Atlantic Wall was a nightmare. It included, among other things, a "devil's delight" of obstacles designed to wreck landing craft—hedgehogs, tetrahedra, Belgian gates, concrete cones, slanting poles topped with mines—the whole draped in barbed wire.
—*Charles B. MacDonald,* The Mighty Endeavor

Omaha Beach—a seven-thousand-yard expanse of sand shaped like a crescent moon on the Calvados coast, or Côte de Nacre (Mother of Pearl)—is remarkable today for its ordinariness and endearing unpretentiousness. But for a few preserved German batteries, a number of museums, the remnants of the "mulberry" (artificial harbor) at Arromanches, some well-placed monuments and a score of illustrated historical plaques, one would hardly know a war took place there sixty-three years ago. This is particularly true of the Vierville sector, where the bloodiest fighting transpired, where the 116th earned everlasting fame.

What's more, given its iconic status in American history, Omaha, too, is rather small. Only at dead-low tide, when the tidal flats stretch more than two hundred yards into the Bay of the Seine, can the beach be called expansive. As the tide comes in, Omaha shrinks away to almost nothing. It is a beach, after all—and is larger than life only in its historical significance.

Likewise, in the 1930s, before Hitler, blitzkrieg and England standing alone, the Côte de Nacre was a resort region of modest means and appeal. And it would remain so today if not for the tourists communing with shadows. Yes, Calvados may be populated by the children of 1944, now sturdy adults, and their descendants, but more so the inhabitants are ghosts, gratitude and memory. In this part of France, at least, the French never forget. The images of men descending from the night sky or pounding ashore in boats on a cloudy morning are indelibly etched on the region's institutional memory and, almost, in its genetic makeup.

But in the winter and spring of 1944, Omaha and the other proposed Allied landing beaches—code-named Utah, Gold, Juno and Sword—

presented a vastly different face. Largely through the efforts of the stern and redoubtable German field marshal Erwin Rommel, the French shoreline had been transformed into a deadly obstacle course choked with mined impediments carefully designed to stymie or throttle even the most ambitious invasion plan.

Rommel, more so than any other German commander, knew that the fate of the Third Reich hung on the Wehrmacht's (or German army's) ability to stop the expected onslaught at its point of origin—on the beaches. It was he who said that the day of invasion—D-Day—would be "the longest day."

So, in addition to heavily mining the shoreline and sinking the hull-ripping obstacles in the Bay of the Seine, the famed Panzer (or tank) commander poured thousands of yards of concrete into bunkers, pillboxes and shore batteries. Likewise, the roads through the draws leading off the beaches were similarly blocked via the liberal use of concrete. And low-lying marsh areas were purposely flooded to check any easy advance should the Allies establish a beachhead.

On the western edge of Omaha, the primary assault area for the companies of the 116th, the natural terrain favored the defenders. The beach, gently sloping and largely open, was backed by an embankment of loose stones, called "shingle," in some places fifteen yards wide.

In the two-thousand-yard sector between the Vierville (D-1) and St. Laurent (D-3) draws, the "shingle" pressed against a seawall—part masonry and part wood—that protected a promenade road. On a beach that offered precious few protective elements, the shingle, which was impassable for vehicles, and the seawall offered some shelter from German mortars and M-26 machine guns. But, as the men of the 116th would soon discover, the problem was getting there.

Beyond the sands, at a distance of a few hundred yards, were scrub-covered bluffs ranging in altitude from 100 feet to 175 feet. From these heights, the defenders could rake the beaches with an enfilading, or sweeping, fire across the length of an assault column.

These bluffs beyond Omaha were cut by five draws, or exits—in essence, the only routes off the beach. Assuming air dominance and a pulverizing pre-invasion artillery barrage, Allied plans called for these draws to be seized by "H-Hour+2," or two hours after the first wave hit the beach. Experience would prove this assumption overly ambitious.

But these Allied plans, in the works for well more than a year, were minutely drawn and governed at their base by lunar and tidal conditions. A night attack, though presented, was summarily dismissed. The main attack would come at dawn, but under what conditions—an ebbing tide or a rising tide?

Landing at low tide meant a long slog over deeply runnelled, or grooved, sands, with German guns trained on those wide tidal flats filled with soldiers. But coming in on a rising tide offered its share of problems as well. For one thing, landing craft would be forced to navigate through and over Rommel's obstacles—the "Belgian gates," the sharply pointed logs aimed seaward, the steel "hedgehogs" (devices sculpted from three metal girders or pieces of rail line welded together at the center), all laced with Teller mines. But the amount of open real estate to be covered by the soldiers before reaching any semblance of shelter would be minimized.

In essence, Allied planners struck a balance. High tides in early June 1944 came in late morning—in fact, at 11:00 a.m. on June 6—so an attack near dawn, on a rising tide, would mean that many of Rommel's impediments would be exposed. But, on the minus side, there would be "no dry landings." Many soldiers, heavily laden with gear, would debark from landing vehicles in water either waist-deep or, in some cases, over their heads.

General Dwight D. Eisenhower, the Allies' supreme commander, originally envisioned June 5 as D-Day, the official start of the invasion. But high wind and rains forced a postponement. On that afternoon, Eisenhower met again with his command staff. The next twenty-four hours offered a break in the weather. The tides would not be conducive again for an invasion for another two weeks, so the fateful decision was made: June 6 it would be.

The attacks would commence the night of June 5. Paratroopers from the U.S. 101st and 82nd Airborne Divisions would drop onto the Cotentin Peninsula beyond Utah Beach (west of Omaha), in the vicinity of the pivotal town of Sainte-Mère-Église.

Likewise, a detachment of the British 6th Airborne, men from the famed 2nd Ox and Bucks (the Oxford and Buckinghamshire Light Infantry) would land Horsa gliders behind Sword Beach and seize vital crossings of the Orne River and the Caen Canal. Minutes after midnight on June 6, they captured the first of these crossings, forevermore known as Pegasus Bridge, in honor of the figure that adorned the shoulder patch worn by the 6th Airborne, a flying horse.

But these operations were antecedent and ancillary to the main event: the storming of the Normandy coast. Through the night of June 5–6, some seven thousand vessels carrying nearly two hundred thousand men—Shep Wohlford among them—quietly made their way across the English Channel to the Bay of the Seine.

The men poised to board the landing craft for the run to the beaches were more than ready for the moment. Though uneasy, they held fast to high expectations. Some ten thousand Allied aircraft would provide cover. An extended artillery barrage, courtesy of the big guns—for instance, of the warship USS *Texas*—would pummel the German defenses.

And so the first wave, many soldiers seasick from the moment they boarded landing craft bobbing up and down in the tossing sea, surged toward Omaha Beach. Some two hundred to three hundred yards from the beach, as J. Robert Slaughter, a Roanoker serving in Company D, recalled in his memoirs, the German artillery began to fire and find its range. At that point, Slaughter remembered realizing, he and his comrades knew it "was not going to be a walk-in. It would be no picnic."

This was particularly true for the soldiers of Company A, many of whom hailed from the small town of Bedford in central Virginia. Attacking along the western edge of Omaha—in the Dog Green sector right in front of the heavily defended Vierville draw—the "Bedford boys" did not have a chance. When the ramp of the vessel carrying company commander Captain Taylor N. Feller—Landing Craft, Assault, No. 1015—dropped down, its thirty-odd inhabitants were cut down, virtually to a man.

The time was 6:36 a.m. The battle for France had begun—and none too auspiciously.

As Harold Baumgarten, a soldier in Company B, noted as he waited for evacuation later that day, "It looked like the beach was littered with the refuse of a wrecked ship that were the dead bodies of what once was the proud, tough and the well-trained combat infantrymen of the 1st Battalion of the 116th Infantry."

The operative watchwords for the rest of that ghastly morning would be *Get off the beach.*

> *The teeming Channel unveiled a dreary dawn, thousands of ships*
> *with artillery drawn; the typhoon weakened, winds abated;*
> *free men prayed and nervously waited.*
> —J. Robert Slaughter, "A New Dawn Awakening"

Technical Sergeant Shep Wohlford and the rest of Company I were in the third wave, slated to go ashore at "H-Hour+50 minutes," or 7:20 a.m. Their scheduled landing sector was Dog Red, slightly west of the hamlet of Les

Moulins, where the D-3 draw led inland to the village of Saint-Laurent-sur-Mer, the company's designated assembly point.

More than likely, Shep, like most, if not all, of the 116th, sailed from England aboard the *Thomas Jefferson*, a fitting name for a ship carrying so many Virginians. At about 3:00 a.m., the men were treated to navy chow—frankfurters and beans, doughnuts and coffee. For some, the meal would be their last.

At 5:00 a.m. or thereabouts, davits lowered the landing craft into the sea, and the men, in full combat gear, scrambled down rope ladders into the tossing vessels. Shep, as a combat infantryman, probably wore his standard olive-drab uniform and a special landing assault jacket. His gear included a standard allotment of M-1 ammunition (sixty rounds, plus three bandoliers around his neck), three fragmentation grenades, a smoke grenade, a phosphorus grenade, a quarter pound of TNT (for blowing foxholes), a day's supply of K rations (three meals) and three chocolate bars, a musette pouch with a tourniquet and a syrette of morphine, an inflatable life preserver called a "Mae West," an amphibious gas mask and—if he smoked—enough cigarettes to get him through the day.

Small wonder, then, that so many survivors of the D-Day ordeal recall the landing craft being too heavily laden to cruise properly through the water. The men themselves were weighed down with a surfeit of equipment.

Company I was divided into six boat teams, two of which were designated assault sections, which essentially meant they would take the lead in finding the company's way off the beach. Each team was supposed to independently fight its way inland, beyond the bluffs, to the assembly point at Saint-Laurent.

The company headed to Omaha alongside the boat teams of Company K, which was scheduled to come ashore at Dog White, just to the west of Dog Red. Both arrived five to ten minutes late, primarily because the strong tide in the Bay of the Seine pushed the boats nearly one thousand yards east of their landing area, well past the D-3 draw. Instead of debarking at Dog Red, Shep and his comrades hit the beach at Easy Green.

The differences in terrain between the two sectors were striking. The bluffs hovering above Dog Red were steeper, but swampy marshland lay between the beach and the double-sloped, terraced bluffs beyond Easy Green.

Companies I and K—with the latter actually landing to the east of Shep and his men—came in bunched together. Fortunately, enemy fire was light—Company K suffered no losses crossing the tidal flat, while Company I sustained but a few casualties—but the beachhead was crowded, as

Company G, which had landed earlier, was still crouched behind the seawall. Thus, unit organization suffered, largely as a result of the boat teams coming ashore virtually on top of each other.

Eventually, small pockets of men began to edge forward, particularly after members of Company I's assault sections breached the barbed wire along an embankment beyond the seawall, using either bangalore torpedoes or, in some cases, mere wire cutters.

It was at this point of the attack that Shep Wohlford, more than likely, suffered his mortal wounds. Establishing a time frame is difficult, but a report in the *Star* of August 11, 1944, states that the twenty-six-year-old died "shortly after landing on the Normandy beachhead."

What is known is that Shep and Staff Sergeant Douglas Orndorff, also of Winchester, took it upon themselves to crawl ahead to scout the German positions. As Orndorff later related to the *Star* while undergoing treatment for a severe eye wound at Valley Forge Hospital near Philadelphia, he and Shep pushed forward because "they wouldn't send their men out to do a job that they wouldn't do themselves."

The two sergeants were hugging the rugged terrain, bullets whistling over their heads, when Shep was hit in the side and stomach. Orndorff reached Shep as he was dying and then, in an effort to complete the mission they had agreed to undertake, crawled ahead about seventy-five yards before a bullet struck him in the face.

Orndorff received first-aid treatment, but the chaotic course of the battle and enhanced German artillery fire forced him to remain on the field for hours before he was transported to a hospital. He lost all sight in his left eye as a result of the wound. Efforts were made at Valley Forge to save the sight in his right eye.

For all the confusion on the beach immediately following the landing, it took but thirty minutes for leading elements of Company I's assault sections to navigate the minefields in the flats beneath the bluffs and then start their ascent. Still, the advance off the beach was decidedly helter-skelter.

For instance, as told in "Omaha Beachhead," part of the "American Forces in Action" series compiled by the U.S. Defense Department, one section leader—possibly Captain Miff Clowe, future mayor of Winchester—moved one hundred yards west of his group's landing area and found a gap in the wire. Signaling for his men to follow, he slipped through the breach and was heading toward the bluffs when he turned to discover that only ten members of his command were behind him. He dispatched a sergeant to find the rest, but the contingent was not seen again for two days. It was later learned they had met stiff German resistance and had fought their way inland toward the assembly area by another route.

This episode is instructive in the manner in which small pockets of "Stonewallers" inched forward from the beach. There were no "charges" per se, merely irregular columns, sometimes in single file, clambering up the heights, checked only by bursts of machine-gun fire or the discovery of minefields.

Eventually, a number of these detachments came together at the top of the bluffs, taking shelter behind a hedgerow two hundred yards farther inland. Few knew their exact location, and many believed they were west, rather than east, of Les Moulins, directly above Dog Red.

Through all this confusion, the boat teams managed to regain their bearings and began to move steadfastly toward Saint-Laurent. By noon, most of Company I had reached the edge of town, five hundred yards beyond the beach, where the road from Les Moulins pinched in at the head of the D-3 draw.

But here the Germans, in company strength, made a stand, seizing high ground that enabled them to maintain a field of fire over open fields, surprisingly uncut by hedgerows, and thus control the approaches to the main crossroads at Saint-Laurent.

And so, for the remainder of the afternoon of June 6 and on into the night, Company I was held at bay, its dogged penetration stalled.

> *Military history has the moral purpose of educating us about past sacrifices that have secured our present freedom and security. If we know nothing of Shiloh, Belleau Wood, Tarawa, and Chosin, the crosses in our military cemeteries are just pleasant white stones on lush green lawns.*
> —*Historian Victor Davis Hanson, "Why Study War?"*

On July 11, five weeks after the 116th Regiment stormed Omaha Beach, the 29th Infantry Division—the lone National Guard outfit in the invasion—dedicated the American cemetery on the heights above those sands of strife.

It is where Shep Wohlford now lies.

On D-Day alone, the 116th lost 608 (341 killed in action, 241 wounded and 26 missing) of its approximately 2,400 men. As a whole, the 29th

"Shep" Wohlford's grave, American Cemetery, Normandy, France. *Courtesy of the O'Connor family.*

Division, over the course of the extended campaign—D-Day until the fall of Germany—suffered 19,814 casualties.

In addressing representatives of the division at the solemn dedication, Major General Charles H. Gerhardt, the 29th's commanding officer, quietly said: "The men that lie here I have seen personally on many occasions on the battlefield. They are comrades in arms and we do honor to their supreme sacrifice for liberty today."

Then, following a burial prayer, the assembled throng sang two hymns, old and familiar, "Abide with Me" and "Nearer, My God to Thee."

Shep was honored as well across the Atlantic when, in fitting tribute to a boy from Bartonsville, the Stephens City Veterans of Foreign Wars post was named for him. And in Winchester, mourning was followed by living, by carrying on.

Sister Marguerite, in May 1941, married Carl Campbell, who had enlisted in the navy directly after Pearl Harbor and served in the Pacific, rising to the rank of chief petty officer. His younger son says with a grin that Carl was forever joking that "he and 'Bull' Halsey won the war [in the Pacific]."

After the war, the Campbells moved back to the Bartonsville homestead and started a family. A boy, Lewis, came first, and then another son, named for his late uncle who died defending freedom on a far-flung beach across the ocean—John Sheppard, or "Shep."

The Campbells moved back to Winchester, where Carl would become postmaster and a longtime high-school football official. They lived first on Clifford Street and then on Stewart Street, next to the apartment building where the Wohlfords resided during the war—Shep's home address at the time of his death. Later, the building was razed to make way for a new surgical clinic, where Marguerite worked as business manager for many years. Talk about a small world—and a small town wonderful in its symmetry of memory.

Just how small was amplified one Election Day back in the 1990s when Shep Campbell, an appointee to city council, was running for election. Standing outside one of the electoral precincts, greeting voters and chatting with friends, Shep could not help but notice two elderly women staring at him. Their gaze was riveted.

Intrigued to the point of inquiry, Shep, currently the president and CEO of Glaize Components, walked over and politely asked the ladies why their eyes were locked in such a way.

"You look just like him," one of the women said. "We never voted for a Republican, but we're voting for you." Shep knew immediately to whom they were referring. And he still smiles at the story.

But he knows, too, that someday he must make the trip, to Omaha Beach and, most especially, to the cemetery atop the bluffs.

More so perhaps than for anybody, the simple white cross in the shade at Plot I, Row 5, Grave 19 waits for him.

Yard by Yard: The Gallant Travails of Douglas Orndorff

They went in by themselves.
That shows a lot about their character.
—Bobby Orndorff

Bobby Orndorff graduated from James Wood High School in 1965, and Shep Campbell from Handley three years later.

Though both men traveled in different circles as teenagers, they knew each other—and of each other—largely through the medium of athletics.

Such is the way in small cities like Winchester.

Bobby was a football star at James Wood and a standout on local baseball and softball diamonds. Shep played basketball on the fine Handley teams of that era. But the two men, still Winchester-area residents, share perhaps a deeper bond—but one neither realized until recently.

Sixty-five years ago today, D-Day, Bobby's father, Douglas, and Shep's uncle (and the man for whom he was named) John Sheppard Wohlford—sergeants together in Company I, 116th Regiment, 29th Infantry Division—crawled forward, away from the hellfire that was Omaha Beach, to scout German positions on the bluffs above the Normandy shore.

Technical Sergeant Wohlford, shot through the side and abdomen, sustained mortal wounds and died where he lay, virtually in the arms of his friend.

Staff Sergeant Orndorff continued to inch forward, yard by agonizing yard, until he, too, was struck by a German bullet…in the face.

Wohlford was buried, along with more than 9,300 other American heroes, in the U.S. military cemetery in Colleville-sur-Mer, France, on those same bluffs overlooking Bloody Omaha.

This is the story of the hero who came home.

Douglas Orndorff. *Courtesy of the Stewart Bell Jr. Archives, Winchester, Virginia.*

Mother, I never felt better in my life. I weigh 186 pounds….
Mother, please don't worry about me. I'll be all right.
—Douglas Orndorff to Vernie Taylor, May 9, 1944

Douglas A. Orndorff, born in Winchester on December 5, 1921, came from a line of bricklayers and stonemasons—and military men.

His father, Charles, laid the brick and stone for a number of distinctive houses on Millwood Avenue in the Greystone Terrace neighborhood. His brother Bruce, known as "Moon," did most of the brickwork on the former F&M Bank.

Orndorff, too, listed his occupation as "bricklayer" when he enlisted in Company I of the 116th Infantry, Winchester's National Guard unit, on October 25, 1940.

Brown-haired and blue-eyed, the five-foot, nine-inch, 175-pounder was inducted into federal service, along with the rest of the company, on February 3, 1941, and assigned to the 29th ("Blue and Gray") Division.

His father, Charles, and stepfather, George Taylor, would also serve during World War II, as would four of his Orndorff cousins—Earl, Joe, Jack and Colleen—whose father, Ernest, fought in World War I.

But Douglas's unit, the 116th, was the one bound for glory and an indelible place in the annals of American warfare. Its companies were among the first to hit Omaha Beach on the cloudy morning of June 6, 1944—D-Day.

For many—341, to be exact—of the 2,400-man 116th, it would be their last day on earth.

Douglas Orndorff, Shep Wohlford and the rest of Company I pounded ashore about 7:30 a.m. in the attack's third wave. Swept along by strong tides in the Bay of the Seine, they hit the beach roughly one thousand yards to the east of their slated landing area, the Dog Red sector of Omaha.

"If a man wasn't scared, there was something wrong with him," Orndorff told the *Star* forty years later.

Other units—Companies G and K, to be precise—suffered the same tide-borne fate. Casualties were light in their impromptu landing area—code-named Easy Green—but the beachhead was jammed with soldiers, and unit organization broke down.

Eventually, small pockets of soldiers began to inch forward, largely because Company I's assault sections had breached the barbed wire strung along an embankment above the beach's seawall. It was at this point, more than likely, that Wohlford and Orndorff decided to slither forward to reconnoiter enemy gun emplacements atop the bluffs.

As the *Star* (then the *Winchester Evening Star*) related on August 11, 1944, following an interview with Orndorff, the two sergeants took this duty upon themselves for a simple reason: "They wouldn't send their men out to do a job that they wouldn't do themselves."

The two men—in reality, little more than boys, as Wohlford was twenty-six and Orndorff a mere twenty-two—were hugging the rugged terrain, machine-gun bullets whistling over their helmets, when Wohlford was hit.

Orndorff managed to reach his comrade as Wohlford's life was slipping away. When his friend died, Orndorff turned forward once again in hopes of completing their mission. "I spotted a German's head," he recalled in the *Star*'s story on the fortieth anniversary of D-Day in 1984. "I can see him yet. He was dug in. I saw him raise his head up."

Orndorff had scrambled seventy-five yards to the base of a hedgerow, had risen to look across and was ready to call for help when a bullet passed through his left eye.

In that same 1984 article, Private Charles Spaid, one of Company I's Browning Automatic riflemen, said that by this time he was "about three to four feet" from Orndorff.

In a 1994 story on the fiftieth anniversary of D-Day, Captain Mifflin B. Clowe, the company commander and later a mayor of Winchester, remembered working his way, accompanied by his radio man, Sergeant Carroll Ashby, to the place where Orndorff lay. Clowe said he didn't recognize his youthful squad leader. "Is that you, Guts?" he recalled asking. Orndorff had acquired that nickname on account of his healthy appetite. "He said, 'Yes,' and asked me for a cigarette. I stuck it between his lips."

Orndorff received immediate first aid, but the German fire was so heavy that stretcher-bearers were unable to get to him for the better part of D-Day. And when they did, he had to survive one last ordeal before leaving Omaha.

As Orndorff reached a boat that would take him to a French field hospital, German fire heated up anew—and, heavily bandaged, he crawled out of the vessel and into the water and hung on to the side for protection.

His "extraordinary heroism in action" earned Orndorff the Distinguished Service Cross and a Purple Heart. The merit citation for the former noted how "he rallied his platoon to attack and, despite the intense enemy fire, fearlessly led them forward in an assault."

A succession of field-hospital stays—the one in France and, later, two in England and another in Scotland—followed until Orndorff, in early July, boarded a ship bound for the United States. Destination: the hospital at New York's Mitchell Field.

He arrived at Mitchell on July 8 and, a week later, was sent to Valley Forge General Hospital in Phoenixville, Pennsylvania. His life was about to change dramatically.

I am getting along all right, still staying in bed.
I can see a little clearer with my eye….This is all I have to say;
don't worry, my eye is coming along all right.
—Douglas Orndorff to Vernie Taylor, August 4, 1944

Orndorff lost that left eye pierced by the German bullet and would regain only 10 percent vision in his right. Thus, it is likely he never truly "saw" the young woman who entered his room—and his life—in Valley Forge.

Anna Mary Vaszily was a dark-haired beauty from Bridgeport, Pennsylvania. She and her sister Margaret visited the hospital frequently to cheer up the wounded veterans.

One day, the sisters stopped in to see a man with his face wrapped in bandages and another with a steel plate in his head—Orndorff and his new best buddy, a Pennsylvanian named Don Steese.

One visit led to another, and to another. As son Bobby says, "Apparently, [my mother] saw something in a one-eyed man." Something enough to accept his proposal to wed. On January 6, 1945, seven months to the day after the landing on Omaha, they left the hospital long enough to be married in the rectory of Our Mother of Sorrows Catholic Church in Bridgeport.

Bobby and his sister Kathy Manuel of Strasburg jokingly refer to this wedding date as "the second D-Day." From the beginning, they say, Douglas and Anna Mary were like "oil and water."

Anna Mary, a first-generation American of Eastern European descent, was deeply religious, a devout Roman Catholic and a city girl to the core. Douglas, whose family had resided in Frederick County for generations, was country, a Protestant and from a military background. They were about as different as two youngsters in love could be.

Tests to the strength of their union came quickly. Upon leaving Valley Forge, Douglas was sent to the Old Farms Convalescent Hospital in Avon, Connecticut. After thirteen weeks of "rehabilitation training"—what we now call occupational therapy—he departed Avon on July 24, 1945, and headed home…without his bride. She followed him.

"The honeymoon was over," Kathy says.

Dad was a survivor, a fighter.
That comes, I suppose, from growing up in the Depression.
—Bobby Orndorff

Though Bobby says his father "had a tough time relating to civilian life," Douglas did anything humanly possible, considering his disability, "to make a dollar and provide for his family."

He was on 100 percent disability status from the army, but that $400 monthly check only went so far, particularly after November 3, 1945, when Bobby was born.

An avid hunter and fisherman, even after the war, Douglas turned to an unlikely trade, at least for these parts: trapping.

In truth, the woods and fields around Winchester teemed with muskrat and mink, otter and fox. Douglas learned the trade from Robert Patton, eleven years his senior but his closest friend since their days playing baseball at old Rouss Park. They would "wheel and deal" their furs, Bobby says, every Saturday at the city's hitching yard on Boscawen Street.

For her part, Anna Mary worked at National Fruit and, for many years, at the A&P store on Amherst Street as a meatcutter.

But a decision made early in their marriage proved to be one of Anna Mary's wisest: She learned to drive—primarily, Bobby says, "so she could keep an eye on [Dad]," who loved to steal away to Charles Town, West Virginia, to play the ponies.

She, in time, learned to love the races, as attested by the "Queen for a Day" celebration at the track on her seventy-fifth birthday. "Dad and Mom," Kathy says, "they worked things out the best they could."

"Oil and water" to the very end.

Dad couldn't drive, and he couldn't really hunt.
But he loved the outdoors….It was said he was one of the best
fishermen on the Shenandoah River.
—Bobby Orndorff

Douglas's disability tempered his personality.

He was a highly disciplined man, largely because he had to be merely to get on in the world. But he could also be distant, withdrawn, particularly with his older child, whom he named for his close friend Robert Patton.

The Orndorffs resided first in what was a veterans' trailer park, on the site of present-day Quarles Elementary School. They later moved to South Kent Street and, finally, in 1952 to Frederick County, on fourteen acres Douglas bought from his mother's kin, the Golightly family. There he was able to plant and tend a large garden.

One day, he asked Bobby to pick some peas. The youngster came back with beans. Douglas growled, "Get out of the garden."

Father and son would occasionally go hunting, which made Bobby nervous—and not because Douglas couldn't see well. In fact, when his father would "hear" a squirrel, Bobby would shoulder the gun, aim it, and Douglas would squeeze the trigger. "I had to make sure I got the hang of it," Bobby says, "because I might not get another shot at going out with him."

Bobby grew into a fine athlete, but, as Kathy says, it "pained and hurt" their father that he could not play catch with his son. He tried but simply could not see the ball. "And so he hardened," Kathy adds.

Nevertheless, Douglas went to all of Bobby's games and stood on the sidelines with a friend alongside to provide commentary. Kathy, born eleven years after Bobby, saw another side of Douglas. "Dad struggled with Bobby as an athlete," she says. "But then I came along, and he became more tender.…I guess I brought out that other side, the compassionate side. He was always there for me."

In 1986, Douglas, then sixty-four, was diagnosed with lung cancer and given three months to live. He had never smoked cigarettes until he entered the service. The habit persisted after the war.

His old friend Don Steese and his wife, Anna Mary's sister Margaret, came down from Pennsylvania to help care for him. He approached death with the same courage he displayed years earlier on Omaha Beach. "He told us, 'I've got this [cancer] so you don't have to,'" Kathy says. "That was his makeup. Then he said, 'Stop that crying.'" On August 16, the end was near, and Douglas knew it.

"I hear the bugles over yonder, calling me home," he said. And then he died. Anna Mary would survive him by eighteen years. She died in 2004.

"He was such a courageous man," Kathy says. "He didn't want to be pitied." True heroes seldom do.

Photographs and Memories

Jean Parker
Rank at D-Day: Corporal
Unit: Women's Auxiliary Air Force
Age at D-Day: 20
Hometown: Melbourne, Australia
Current Residence: Bunker Hill, West Virginia
Occupation: Proprietor, the Australian Store

"I was a member of the Women's Australian Auxiliary Air Force. I was a wireless telegraphist specialist under the command of the Royal Australian Air Force. We were the RAAF headquarters for the South Pacific. General [Douglas] MacArthur wrote that we knew more war secrets than he did.

"I cannot recall anything particular [about D-Day]…other than we had been on standby for two weeks and all leave had been cancelled. We

Howard Allen of Winchester reads the *Winchester Evening Star* in a European foxhole. *Courtesy of the Stewart Bell Jr. Archives, Winchester, Virginia.*

knew that something big was on, but then, in the South Pacific war theater something big was old hat to us. We just hoped each time a flap was on that it was to be the last one and we could all go home."

Earle "Bill" Parker
Rank at D-Day: Corporal
Unit: 1st Marine Division
Age at D-Day: 26
Hometown: Jersey City, New Jersey
Current Residence: Bunker Hill, West Virginia
Occupation: Retired automotive engineer

"I was…serving in the South Pacific. We had just come home from the Russell Islands to recuperate from the campaign in North Britain and prepare for the upcoming campaign in the Paleu Islands. The information we got was news briefs from a radio that the landing had taken place. Our thoughts and prayers were with those blokes as I knew firsthand what they had faced. I had been at Guadalcanal."

CHARLES E. WATERMAN
Rank at D-Day: Corporal
Unit: 286th Joint Assault Signal Company
Age at D-Day: 23
Hometown: Danville, Illinois
Current Residence: Shenandoah Valley Westminster-Canterbury in
   Winchester
Occupation: Reporter, screenwriter, speechwriter, public affairs officer.
   Semi-retired with small company, conducting public speaking and
   writing seminars.

What follows is a series of excerpts from "Corporal's Eye View: June 6, 1944, D-Day, Utah Beach," written by Charles E Waterman.

"It's dark when we arrive at a wooded area. The word is passed we are to prepare a will and write a letter home, but it won't be mailed for about two weeks.

"Our briefing room is poorly lit on a huge wall map. I understand the military symbols.

"A captain goes over the map: 'Red Beach', 'Green Beach, 'Yellow Beach'. The name of the operation? 'OVERLORD' Our landing area? 'Utah Beach'.

"I turn to a buddy. 'So this is our maneuver plan!'

"'Hell no. This is the invasion!' It hardly seems to be the place to ask, what about some training before I face a real enemy?

"We are aboard an LCI [landing craft infantry]. It's only about 125 feet long and flat bottom for shallow beaches. That means it's not stable in this heavy sea.

"On deck, the view is incredible—ships around us, for 360 degrees. Some have large barrage balloons. It's dark and wet and cold. I go below....

"It's now a little before 4:00 a.m., the sixth of June. We are in full pack, with rifles. I expect to see our little ship drive up on the French shoreline and all of us rush out, as in the newsreels.

"But my company is ordered over the gunwale and down a net. The first troops are dropping off into what looks to me like an oversized horsed trough, which is pitching violently.

"My turn comes. I swing over the side, struggling to keep my rifle and buckles from hanging up in the net.

"We are the fourth wave. First, the underwater demolition teams had looked for underwater obstacles. Double crossed the railroad rails, looking like monstrous jacks, stick up out of the surf, robbed of their explosives (we hope).

"Next were infantry troops.

"Third, our guys from the 1st Engineer Special Brigade of the 4th Division: they're the ones with the bulldozers. They could be building a townsite, the way they handled their heavy equipment. I decide there's a hero's job.

"Fourth is my own 286. We're to set up and operate communications for the whole landing.

"Low Commands, and then a thud and a scraping sound. The heavy ramp falls, and men up front start out, more gingerly than I'd seen in the movies.

"My turn: 'Hey noncom,' tells me to grab a reel of field wire. It weighs perhaps fifty pounds. I'd just as soon not have this additional weight, but I lug it along.

"The step down is surprisingly deep, above my waist, my boots seek firm places. The sun isn't up yet. The quietness of my comrade is eerie.

"My new amphib boots scuff dry sand. I'm on Utah Beach in Normandy, France.

"It's perfectly still in the thick morning mist. I'm about sixth in line, and there's been just one set of tracks in the dewy grass.

"'Pssst! Step in their tracks, stupid!'

"'Why?' I ask, giving vent to perhaps the most unwanted philosophical question of the day.

"'Landmines!'

"The pre-battle augmentation notion is taking on meaning for me.

"The fog thins for a moment. To my right, within stumbling distance, lies a young soldier, face up. There's a hole in the man's forehead the size of a man's fist. My first man dead.

"Was he German or American? At this writing, I honestly don't know. But it's been some 18,200 days now, and I still sweep my hand across my forehead when I'm nervous."

WILLIAM S. FUNKHOUSER
Rank at D-Day: Sergeant
Age at D-Day: 20
Hometown: Fisher's Hill
Current Residence: Strasburg
Occupation: Retired from Avtex

As Bill Funkhouser best remembers, more than four hundred men (including replacements) fought with Company F at some point during D-Day. Of this four hundred, he says but four—himself being one—made it through the "Longest Day" without being hit.

The Morning: "They woke us up at 4:30 a.m. We got an apple and a cup of coffee. I don't remember eating anything else the rest of the day.…

"It was just daylight and the beach looked foggy and smoky. It was a long way off in the ship for firing in on the beach before we landed. They had a new kind of shell; we had never seen anything like it before. It fired and then, all at once, it looked like a whole swarm of blackbirds flying to the beach and they all fell at the edge of the water and exploded."

The Landing: "The water there was just about knee deep. I thought to myself, 'Maybe I won't get very wet,' but as we made our way in, it got deeper and deeper. I was afraid it was going to get over my head, so I inflated my life preserver.…

"I remember one boy beside me lost his helmet. He was reaching for it, but the waves kept pushing it away. It was floating over to me, so I caught it and gave it back to him. We separated it, and all of a sudden, they [the Germans] knocked him down with machine-gun fire. He got up and they knocked him down again. He got up a second time they knocked him down for the third time, for good."

On the beach: "I started crawling and got out of the water. A guy on my left was carrying TNT. I don't know what set it off, but there was a big white flash. It scattered him all across the beach in front of me. I couldn't crawl through that mess, so I got up to run. But when I jumped up my legs wouldn't hold me and I fell right back down. I thought that machine-gun fire that went over my legs in the water had hit me.

"I couldn't wait for the waves to wash the remains of that boy in front of me away because I knew I would have soon been dead, so I just shut my eyes and crawled as fast and as far as I could. I stopped behind a post. A bullet came through that post and it fell right in front of me in the sand. I was going to pick it up and put it in my pocket for a souvenir, but I picked it up and it burned my fingers and I thought 'You fool.' So I rolled over and crawled on in to dig it in. I didn't want to raise up to get my shovel off my pack, so I just used my hands.

"I had no idea what time it was. That day seemed like it lasted for weeks.

"Eventually, Captain Finkey called out 'F company moving out,' and we passed the word along. We went back down along the beach and it was just solid in the surf—dead guys washing back and forth in the waves all the way up. We started up over a hill and the captain sent me and Patty Fagan and one other guy out as scouts.

The 116th Infantry Regiment drills at Fort Meade, Maryland. *Courtesy of the Stewart Bell Jr. Archives, Winchester, Virginia.*

Virginia Woolen Company employees pose outside POW camp near Virginia Avenue Elementary School in Winchester. *Courtesy of the Stewart Bell Jr. Archives, Winchester, Virginia.*

Captain Mifflin Clowe (*right*), future mayor of Winchester, receives military commendation after D-Day. *Courtesy of the Stewart Bell Jr. Archives, Winchester, Virginia.*

"We went and machine gunfire opened up on us, so we hit the ground. I started crawling out along a field and a line of machine gunfire came down in the dirt right beside me. So I rolled the other way and let my rifle lay. I told Patty to fire down into the corner where I thought it came from. They didn't return fire, so we jumped up and ran to the edge of the field where there was a ditch by a high hedge. I lay down and saw that my pants were changing color by my hip. I thought I had been hit but what had happened was that my canteen was shot right through the top."

Virgil L. Miller
Rank at D-Day: Technician Fourth Grade (Sergeant)
Unit: 4th Signal Company, 4th Infantry Division
Age at D-Day: 25
Hometown: Baker, West Virginia
Current Residence: Frederick County
Occupation: Retired government worker, U.S. Department of Defense

"I landed in the ETO [European Theater of Operations] on January 30, 1944. We were in camp in Tiverton, England. I read several stories about the Invasion of June 6. It was scheduled for June 4, June 5 or June 6. The weather was bad, period; if the sixth was too bad for the operation, it would have to wait until weather was suitable.

"I did not go in on D-Day, but on D-6. I think I was in a boat on the channel waiting for beachheads to be established."

Henry Regenthal
Rank at D-Day: Private
Unit: 5th Amphibious Special Brigade (Engineers)
Age at D-Day: 19
Hometown: Newark, New Jersey
Current Residence: Stephens City
Occupation: Retired toolmaker

"I was with the Fifth Amphibious Engineering Brigade going in on an LCT. I was sitting on two thousand pounds of satchel charges, used for blowing up beach obstacles from the third assault wave and watching all the fireworks.

"I thought to myself, I'd rather be fishing."

Edward F. Chapman
Rank at D-Day: Sergeant
Unit: Battery A, 397th Antiaircraft Artillery Battalion, 49th Antiaircraft
   Artillery Brigade
Age at D-Day: 23
Hometown/Current Residence: Boyce
Occupation: Railroad employee, Fruit Growers Express

"I was in Normandy in the invasion of France, June 6, 1944, on Omaha Beach. The picture is etched in my mind and will be there until the end.

   "There's not much of a story to tell in a few words. I was on the beach for four days. My outfit was scattered all along the beach.

   "I helped the medics recover bodies from the beaches—one job I'll never forget. I was asked to pick up weapons off the beach and repair them for the ground troops coming ashore."

Note: The 397th was commended by General George C. Marshall, Chief of Staff, for its "personal bravery, gallantry, professional skill, and complete devotion to duty in the face of overwhelming odds." From Lieutenant Colonel Leslie J. Staub, commander of the 397th, Sergeant Chapman received this note: "Your arduous duties were performed in the face of terrific obstacles and contributed to the success of the assault on D-Day. I sincerely appreciate your efforts and commend you for your performance which reflects great credit upon yourself and the highest traditions of the military service."

Steve Theron
Rank at D-Day: Private First Class (Rifleman and then Signal Corps
   radioman)
Age at D-Day: 18
Hometown: London, Ontario, then Washington, D.C.
Current Residence: Berryville
Occupation: Restaurant and mobile-home park owner, now employed
   by Walmart

"Yes, I was there in on the invasion on D-Day....It's not nice to see your buddies drop around you. But what I would like to talk about are two important events that took place in France and Germany that were the

Crosses in American Cemetery, Colleville-sur-Mer, Normandy, France. *Courtesy of the O'Connor family.*

highlights of my tour through France, Belgium, Luxembourg and, finally, Germany itself.

"1. The meeting of Winston Churchill, General Eisenhower, General Montgomery and General George S. Patton, all together with General George C. Marshall.

"2. I saw George S. Patton take off his overshoes and give them to a GI on the front line. To me, George S. Patton was a soldier's general in every sense of the word."

Katherine Mull
Rank at D-Day: Technician Fourth Grade (Sergeant)
Unit: XIX District Engineers in Taunton, England
Age at D-Day: 24
Hometown: Baldwin, Long Island, New York
Current Residence: Fredrick County
Occupation: Retired intelligence operations specialist, U.S. Department
of Defense

"From February 1942 to July 1957, I was on active military duty. As a T/4 (Sergeant) from April 1944 to September 1944, I was stationed in Taunton, England, with the XIX District Engineers, preparing land maps and briefs on areas on the continent for future use by Allied forces.

"During May 1944, working hours were at a high level and our entire unit was in some form of military training to be used at a later date. For the women, this included arms training, a scaled-down martial arts [self-defense] training and chemical warfare familiarization.

"We all knew that 'THE' day was imminent. On the morning of June 6, 1944, our entire area was bombarded with thousands of leaflets bearing General Dwight D. Eisenhower's signature, announcing that this was, indeed, 'D-Day.' The feeling of accomplishment, a reward for our months of preparation, had finally reached a climax! It was a thrill, even an honor to know that we really were a part of history in the making.

"The months and years to follow verified this, and it is a moment in my life I shall never forget."

Sam McCall
Rank at D-Day: Corporal
Unit: Company C, 116th Infantry Regiment, 29th Infantry Division
Age at D-Day: 21
Hometown: Harrisonburg
Current Residence: Winchester
Occupation: Retired from Lance Products

"I enlisted in the armed forces on February 4, 1941, in the 116th Infantry, 29th Division at Fort Meade, Maryland. We had set up camp at South Hill on December 7, 1941, when Pearl Harbor was attacked. In September of 1942, we left New York on the *Queen Mary*, destined for Scotland. We loaded on trains and were shipped to southern England. A year later we were shipped to Ivory Bridge, England.

"Was it luck or destiny?

"I had to be admitted to the hospital there for medical reasons when the secret day arrived, D-Day, June 6, 1944. Seven days later I was sent back to my company at Omaha Beach at Normandy, France. The great offensive took me through France, Belgium, Holland and Germany. We were on the Elbe River just outside of Berlin when the war ended in 1945."

EDWIN A. CUBBY
Rank at D-Day: Captain
Unit: 88th Replacement Battalion
Age at D-Day: 28
Hometown: Little Falls, New Jersey
Current Residence: Shenandoah Valley Westminster-Canterbury in
    Winchester
Occupation: Retired professor of social studies, Marshall University,
    Huntington, West Virginia

"Weeks before June 6, there was an increase in military activity in our area [Warminster in Wiltshire, England], but not enough to cause anxiety or arouse curiosity. For example, we were ordered to send a 'package of replacements' to the 23rd Infantry Regiment, which was undergoing training on the coast of Wales near Tenby Bay….I wondered, 'Why way out there?'

"Three of my Syracuse fraternity brothers became aware via letters from my wife [Claire] and their mothers, of each other's presence in the same part of England. By good fortune the four of us were able to meet on a Sunday near Stonehenge. Being stationed at Tidworth were officers in the 2nd Armored Division. The fact that our paths had crossed where and when they did gave us a sense that something big must be in the works.

"Within two weeks of our chance meeting, Operation Overlord began. My friends in the 2nd Armored made the D-Day crossing and survived the ordeal and incidentally, are alive and well in Syracuse, New York.

"As I remembered June 6, the skies were clear over southern England. Nothing seemed unusual as we went about our usual task until sometime during the morning when we became aware of activity overhead. A large number of planes, not in formation, seemed to be circling. They appeared to be Dakotas and/or two-engine bombers, which led to speculation as to why they were there. Was it a rendezvous or were they circling while waiting for landing instructions? Later in the day, the radio began reporting what was actually going on. I can't recall any expression of exuberance; rather, I think the mood was one of solemnity as we returned to our normal duties."

MARY WELLES PEARSON
Job at D-Day: American Red Cross staff assistant
Current Residence: Shenandoah Valley Westminster-Canterbury in
    Winchester

"In spite of air raids, bombed-out families, buzz bombs, many of us saw some lighter moments during World War II. After all, I was sent to England to build morale, nothing else.

"It was at the 8th Air Force headquarters [at High Wycombe, near Norwich, England] that I first laid eyes on the man who eventually became my husband—my own morale-builder.

"Arriving in England convinced that 1943 was the worst possible time for any but the most casual relationships with men, I had been there one week when I met him. He was a staff sergeant at the 8th Bomber Command at High Wycombe. He never told any secrets, but he knew everything that was going on, as he worked in the operations room, having daily conferences with the air force generals, sending out the orders to the bomber wings and receiving back the results of the raids on the continent.

"After having had some dinner dates, late one afternoon he appeared with two rented bicycles so we could ride in the lovely Buckinghamshire countryside. When darkness fell, we stopped to rest on the top of the hill. After some lighthearted conversation, he made his first pass at me, which I found remarkably pleasant.

"There were some funny noises coming from a spot nearby, but I was too engrossed to give them any thought. Imagine my surprise, after a while, when I realized our romantic encounter was taking place beside a pigpen!

"On D-Day, my sergeant and I arranged to meet in London. Usually a prompt person, he was two hours late, and his first words were, 'Come on, we're getting out of London now.' All American personnel knew something was happening, because for several days we had been required to carry our gas masks. But many of us didn't know why, and those 'in the know' never told us anything.

"Soon the bus bomb started arriving and I then understood why John wanted to get out of London so fast."

CARPER W. BUCKLEY
Rank at D-Day: Second Lieutenant
Unit: 433rd Counterintelligence Corps
Age at D-Day: 33
Hometown: Clifton
Current Residence: Shenandoah Valley Westminster-Canterbury
Occupation: Superintendent of documents, Government Printing
    Office, Washington, D.C.

"Regarding D-Day, I can contribute very little, I was at Camp Barnes, just outside the city of Noumea on the island of New Caledonia in the South Pacific. As we went for our evening meal, someone passed by in a jeep and told us that the invasion was underway. There was a minimum of horn-blowing and feeble attempts at some sort of celebration, but mostly a somber reaction, realizing the tremendous loss of life that was inevitable. All of us in the Pacific area also knew that, after everything was concluded in Europe, there was still the invasion and final defeat in Japan, in which we would most likely be directly involved."

EVE JONES
Age at D-Day: 14
Hometown: London
Current Residence: Stephens City
Occupation: Housekeeper, Shenandoah Valley Westminster-Canterbury
    in Winchester

Eve Jones had a firsthand view of World War II as a youngster in London. Among her remembrances are the following:
    The Battle of Britain: "I remember one particular Saturday when it was at its height. There were many, many dogfights overhead…pilots were bailing out and we would watch them parachute down. The enemy—we mild-mannered Britishers were pretty angry and were ready to meet them with pitchforks. This was the day that the most enemy planes were shot down. That night, as night fell, the area toward the London docks the sky was red, lit up with the burning buildings. We felt very vulnerable."
    Dunkirk: "This was when the little boats, the paddle steamers went across the English Channel to bring back the troops. I remember the stories and the radio requests for those who had seaworthy boats to rescue the troops."

The Blitz: "This again was a vulnerable time period; the air-raid warnings were mostly at night. Moonlit nights were bombers' moons. Nightly air raids became routine. The blackout was secured.…Sometimes we would listen to propaganda from Germany, the program *Germany Calling with Lord Haw Haw*. You listen for the planes and bombs—the bombs, if they rattled as they fell, no worry; but if they whistled, you dove under the kitchen table.

"The war years continued. We found that we could get used to almost anything—the rationing, the shortages, the bombing. We found we still had our sense of humor and that indomitable spirit. With the leadership of Sir Winston Churchill, who could only offer blood, sweat, toil and tears—and 'We will fight them on the beaches, in the streets, etc.'—we would win.

The build-up to D-Day: "Near where I lived there was some open common ground [actually a part of the Epping Forest]. The road bordering this land had enormous horse chestnut trees and oaks lining it. Camouflage convoys of troops and materials would regularly come through from the north and stay during the day and move out overnight for the southern ports. With the help of the U.S. and all other gallant nations, at last the tides of war had changed, had turned. We knew that there would be an invasion of continental Europe, but where and when? We know that it was Normandy, and June 6, 1944. It, for me, was a lot of my growing years, but we knew at last, to quote our leader, 'It was not the end, but the beginning of the end.'"

Nancy Larrick Crosby
Job at D-Day: Editor and education director, education section of the
    War Savings Division, U.S. Department of the Treasury
Age at D-Day: 34
Hometown: Winchester
Current Residence: Shenandoah Westminster-Canterbury in
    Winchester
Occupation: Retired writer and editor of children's literature

"One job [I had] was to explain the why and how of children's aid in the war effort through their purchase of war saving stamps and bonds and the conservation of resources. It proved to be an extremely effective way to reach parents in the public in general.

"My primary job was to edit a quarterly eight-page newsprint tabloid for every schoolchild—literally every child. It reported news from various communities, suggestions for classroom projects, usually a poster done by an outstanding children's book illustrator.

"I visited the War Savings office in almost every state gathering news, speaking at pep rallies, and meeting with school groups. I also addressed many professional organizations of teachers and recruited their help in preparing and distributing teachers' guides, such as lessons in saving, interest rates, etc. for arithmetic classes.

"It was a heady time!"

CARL B. LEE
Rank at D-Day: C-5 Corporal Technician
Unit: 29th infantry, 175th Regiment Headquarters Company
Age at D-Day: 22
Hometown: Delray, West Virginia
Current Residence: Echo Village
Occupation: Retired carpenter at Howard Shockey and Sons Inc.

"It was a funny feeling, not knowing what was in front of you, not knowing what could happen next," Lee says of the weight in a Landing Ship, Tank, before the D-Day invasion. "We had a great view of the beach; we could see everything; and we knew we had to make that journey before long."

Hollywood actress Greer Garson attends War Bonds rally in Winchester. Future Mayor Charles Zuckerman stands to Miss Garson's left. *Courtesy of the Stewart Bell Jr. Archives, Winchester, Virginia.*

Before the invasion, Lee spent most of his time waterproofing a jeep for the invasion. "Anywhere saltwater could get in was covered with a mixture of rubber." When the ramp dropped on the LST on D-Day+1, "You took off, you kept going…there was no time to play around." The LST dropped the jeeps in the water so deep that it almost "came over the top of the jeep."

"I drove that jeep in England and to the end of the war," he said.

Lee was among the 29th Division troops that ended the war at the Elbe River; on the opposite bank was the Russian army.

2

ANZIO INVADERS

Dick Kern's Decision

I never had any infantry training,
but that's what I ended up fighting as—an infantryman.
—Richard D. "Dick" Kern

When Dick Kern graduated from Virginia Tech—then VPI—in the spring of 1942, he faced a critical decision: play professional football or enter military service as a newly minted second lieutenant.

A standout quarterback at VPI, Kern (Handley, class of 1938) had offers to play pro ball. The Philadelphia Eagles wanted him, and so did the Detroit Lions. But for him, like millions of other young men of that era, a rather seminal event in the fall of his senior year, at a military installation named Pearl Harbor, had changed his life—and America's attitude toward the war engulfing Europe and the Far East.

"People in America, obviously, were not wanting to get in," says Kern, still robust at ninety-one. "But when the Japanese hit Pearl Harbor, there was a complete change of attitude."

But the future car dealer and city councilman still had a choice to make. He assessed the situation realistically. Sure, he could resign his commission and play in the NFL. But that fledgling career would last a year, maybe two, before Uncle Sam inevitably called, a draft notice in hand. So, he thought, if the future held the definite promise of military service, why not go in as an officer?

Dick Kern. *Courtesy of the Stewart Bell Jr. Archives, Winchester, Virginia.*

And so, as a member in good standing of VPI's Corps of Cadets, he walked across a stage where commencement officials handed out "commissions in one hand and orders in the other."

Kern's first stop: Virginia's Camp Eustis. Then it was on to Camp Hulen in Texas for anti-aircraft training, an extension of the instruction he had received while a cadet in Blacksburg.

Unlike his buddies—and former National Guard colleagues—from Winchester whose first whiff of combat came in the hellfires of D-Day, Kern saw action in America's first major offensive, in North Africa. And just getting to the shores of Algeria proved a crucible in itself. On their way to the port of Oran, a German U-boat attacked his troopship.

"You're nervous all the time to begin with," he says. "My men were in the hull, and the minute an attack started, I was supposed to go where my men were. It was nerve-wracking, sitting on the steps going down into the hull and knowing a submarine was trying to put a torpedo in my lap."

After that episode, North Africa proved relatively uneventful. Kern's field artillery unit—attached to the 34th Infantry Division for anti-aircraft protection—initially guarded the small Algerian town of Beni Saf, with its iron-ore mines.

Kern then led his 190-man company to a base featuring P-38 Lightning aircraft and, while there, received orders to return to Oman. Their next port of call: Italy.

The Allies had already invaded and conquered Sicily when Kern and his gunners shipped out. When reminded today that he could just as easily have been preparing for D-Day with so many of his friends from Winchester, Kern says, simply, "I had my own D-Day. I was at Anzio."

When the 34th Division joined the fight around that famous beachhead in March 1944, Kern and his mates were still artillery men. That would soon change.

With foot soldiers at a premium and German airpower diminished. General Mark Clark, commander of the U.S. 5th Army, formed an infantry regiment from five anti-aircraft battalions. Among the units so transformed was Dick Kern's. His real war was only beginning.

Dick Kern's Request

On the front lines, there's a veneer of civilization,
a very thin one—and it soon rubs off.
—Richard B. "Dick" Kern

Captain Dick Kern landed in Italy, at the fabled Anzio beachhead, as a relatively untried artillery officer. The former Handley High football star left the battle-scarred, boot-shaped peninsula a seasoned combat leader— of infantry.

With German airpower in the Italian sector diminished and his own need for foot soldiers heightened, General Mark Clark, commander of the U.S. 5th Army, quickly transformed five anti-aircraft battalions into the 473rd Infantry Regiment. Kern's artillery unit was one of those so affected.

And by "quick transformation," Kern, in relating the story of those 1944 days, means just that. "We had a lieutenant assigned to our company for about two weeks," he says. "He gave us what training we had…and then we were put in the line as infantry.

"None of us had been trained as infantry. It was like taking a bunch of men here in Winchester and going into the line as infantry."

Making the transition even more daunting, Kern says, was the fact that a crack German unit—the all-volunteer 16th SS Division—stood in their path, giving ground ever so grudgingly up the boot.

"They were among their best troops," Kern says. "They trained us the hard way."

As newly minted foot soldiers, Kern and his men were hardly immune to error. For instance, as the unit was gaining a foothold in Pisa after attacking across the Arno River, Kern recalls one of his sergeants looking at the city's famed Leaning Tower and saying, "Let's put Old Glory on top."

"I said, 'Wow, that's good. Do it.' But we were fighting house-to-house, and when we did that, they [the Germans] knew exactly where we were. We started getting artillery fire. I realized I had made a mistake."

In the tense fighting, the Germans, Kern says, managed to place observers in the Leaning Tower who directed gunners to rain shot and shell on him and his men. He radioed headquarters "requesting" that fire be directed at the world-renowned landmark.

"I didn't think the Tower was worth one of my men," he says. "So I requested—I did not order—fire. But I was told 'No', that it was a safe zone. At the time, I felt my men were more valuable than the Leaning Tower."

The Italian people, Kern says, did all they could to help the Allies. One day during the Pisa campaign, a woman stopped Kern and his men as they started to cross a "field of wheat." She wanted to tell them a big house looming in the distance was an enemy command post. So Kern pulled his men back and asked for artillery assistance.

"We started shelling the house," he says, "really hitting it well. The Germans abandoned the house, and started back across the field. And my men started flushing out Germans, flushing 'em out like they were birds."

In the fog of war, some Germans tried to surrender. They "came out," so Kern recalls, "with their hands up. But my men were so tense that as many as twenty or thirty more shots were fired."

One enemy soldier, he says, suffered a leg wound, and about seven others "were pretty badly wounded." So Kern and his men carried the Germans about one hundred yards back toward the rear "so an ambulance could get to them."

One of his sergeants spoke German, he remembers, and said, "Captain, let me handle this." Kern paid him no heed. "He would have killed them," he says.

Hence that "veneer of civilization" soon rubbed off.

Dick Kern's Lucky Day

We didn't have the [infantry] *training, but I can't say enough*
good things about the American soldier as a fighter.
They were great.
—Richard B. "Dick" Kern

Dick Kern is ninety-one years young and so has lived a lot of days. But one in particular, from his time as a combat soldier in World War II, he remembers as his "luckiest."

Funny, but even before that tumultuous day near a canal along the west coast of Italy, Kern considered himself fortunate. By that juncture, he had escaped major bodily harm save for minor wounds sustained south of Pisa and was the last captain standing of four from the day his artillery outfit was made an infantry unit.

Kern, by then, had also run into two buddies from home: Gene Dunn, with whom he'd played football at Handley, and Ralph Shafer.

A bedraggled Sergeant Dunn, informed that a captain was looking for him, expected anyone but Kern—most likely an officer eager to reprimand him for his role in a spirited "altercation" near Naples. When he saw Kern, he didn't know him. His friend had grown a moustache.

And, finally, following a spirited tussle for Pisa, Kern and his unit advanced up the Italian Riviera. He recalls staying "in a different hotel each night." Life, for this infantryman, was relatively good.

In fact, on the day he stopped his men by the side of that canal, Kern "hadn't seen a German" in hours. And so, he says, he got "a little careless," huddling with his junior officers in a "bunch."

"I gave them a target," he says.

Machine-gun fire, aimed too high, ripped through tree leaves above Kern's head. His men scrambled for cover inside a house. He stayed outside and vividly recalls bullets pinging off the tanks assigned to his unit.

German gunners then zeroed in on Kern and his men with artillery. "I knew," Kern says, "I had to get to my own artillery and fire back." To do so required radio contact, and Kern was far from his radioman.

What commenced then was a deadly game of "catch me if you can"— Kern racing from house to house when he sensed German machine- gunners had stopped firing to cool their weapons.

He scurried around to the back of a home only to be confronted by an eight-foot wall, which he scaled—only then to see a wire and the telltale skull and crossbones. He had dropped into a minefield.

"I had to get across that field to get to my radio," he says. "So I jumped from clod to clod, and studied the ground all the way. I got across…by the grace of God."

Given directions amid the "chaos" by an Italian who spoke English, Kern found his way back to his radio and provided the proper coordinates for artillery fire.

And so ended the action part of the "luckiest" day of his life.

But Kern's fighting days were far from over. In the struggle for imposing Mount Belvedere, "in front of Bologna," his company attacked and then, all but isolated when the company on its left was overrun, held firm in the face of a fierce counterassault. The 10th Mountain Division then marched to their relief. "It took them, a whole division, two months to take [Belvedere]," Kern says, noting his company had initially been given that order.

Kern came home in 1945 and, told to report to Fort Bragg, thought he was bound for the Pacific. But President Truman dropped two atomic bombs on Japan, thus ending the war.

An industrial engineer by training, Kern took a job with American Viscose in Front Royal. He was there but a short while when his father applied for, and gained, a franchise to sell Kaiser-Frazier autos.

So Dick Kern started selling cars. That was sixty-five years ago. And to an office at that Valley Avenue dealership he still comes today.

Remembering Raleigh

Raleigh Easter would have turned eighty-one this coming Saturday. He may have spent the day quietly with family; or visiting his fellow vets at the Veterans Administration hospital in Martinsburg, West Virginia; or perhaps even throwing a line in the water at the Isaak Walton pond off US 50.

There were few things Easter liked better than fishing, except perhaps helping folks, particularly the men reduced to a life of endless days and monotony at VA hospitals. And, in the end, he would learn a little about that, too.

Raleigh passed his last eighteen months up in Martinsburg, at the very facility where he amassed certificate after certificate for volunteer hours. Though declared 100 percent disabled in 1980 and in frequent pain himself, he pushed wheelchairs, gave rides to and from the hospital and wrote countless letters to legislators and even to the White House on behalf of vets. On April 4 of this year, he died in these familiar surroundings.

Upon seeing his obituary in the *Star*, I instantly regretted that, in the nine years this column has known print, I had never taken the time to know one of the Winchester area's more decorated World War II soldiers.

It wasn't as if he were not around. As a commander of the local VFW post, a longtime member of its honor guard and a driving force in the erection of an armed services monument at Shenandoah Memorial Park, Raleigh was never particularly far from the news.

Fortunately, I had occasion to receive an email from his family—particularly son Dan and daughter-in-law Sharon—asking us to insert a note of thanks in our Letters column to all who participated in or attended his funeral service. I wrote back, inquiring about the possibility of a column about their "Dad."

Schedules conflicted—little did I know that Dan and Sharon reside in Newport News—and meetings were put off, until last Saturday. Then I "met" Raleigh Easter for the first time, through spoken memories and a voluminous scrapbook of clippings, photos and official papers.

Not only did I learn (anew) that he was a fine soldier—and that he saved everything—but also that he was perhaps a better person. Wounded three times as an infantryman in the 3rd Division, Raleigh, son Dan says, "was not the same person when he came back" from the war.

He could still work—which he did as an industrial electrician—but when his three sons were growing up, he was unable to toss a baseball with them. Angry at the army for issuing him an honorable discharge for medical reasons, he satisfied what can only be described as a continuing hunger for service by pouring himself into community work, more often than not with a veterans-oriented twist.

"He did a lot for the community," Dan, himself a career navy man, says. "That was his way of giving back." As if the valorous deeds that earned him two Silver Stars, three Bronze Stars and two Purple Hearts were not enough.

More so than even most members of the "greatest generation," World War II was a transforming experience for Raleigh. He left the farm on which he grew up southwest of Stephens City a fresh-faced eighteen-year-old who walked everywhere and wanted to be a meatcutter. He returned a warrior, upset that he could not make the army his career.

But in a special way, he did, as attested by a lifetime of devotion and commitment to his fellow comrades in arms.

"Helluva Fighting Man"

Perhaps the first indication of the kind of soldier Raleigh Dayton Easter, late of Winchester, would become came on his very first day in the army in the summer of 1943.

As his son Dan tells it, Raleigh was in line to receive his uniforms and equipment when a GI, measuring feet for combat boots, performed his duties, let us say, a tad too rigorously. Raleigh responded by "knocking [the man] out cold." The sergeant in charge quickly waded into the fray to reprimand Raleigh, who told him, "You do the same thing and I'll cold-cock you."

Raleigh Easter. *Courtesy of the Stewart Bell Jr. Archives, Winchester, Virginia.*

Taken aback, the sergeant said, "Give this man whatever he wants. He'll be a helluva fighting man."

Dan swears the story is true, and there's no reason to doubt him, as his dad, in time, would prove that sergeant right. As an infantryman in the 2nd Battalion, 7th Regiment, 3rd Division, serving in Italy and France, Raleigh would earn two Silver Stars, three Bronze Stars and two Purple Hearts. He *was* a "helluva fighting man."

Perhaps it was in his genes. Raleigh's dad, Shadrick, chased Pancho Villa along the Mexican border with "Black Jack" Pershing in 1916 and then saw combat in France during World War I.

Or maybe it can be attributed to an ornery disposition. As Dan's wife, the former Sharon McCoy of Frederick County, says, her father-in-law was a bit of a "hell-raiser" in his day.

Dan provides further testimony to this notion. One evening in France, he told me two Saturdays ago, Raleigh and a buddy entered a bar in search of liquid refreshment. They were refused service and asked to leave.

"We're defending your country and you don't want me here?" Raleigh said, firing his sidearm into the ceiling. "Well, you can just keep your country and send me back to the beautiful Shenandoah Valley of Virginia."

That happened, of course, but not until Raleigh distinguished himself on the field of battle, thrice suffering wounds that would earn him that trip home on a hospital ship.

He was nineteen years old when he hit the Italian beaches in 1944. He sustained his first wound, courtesy of a German tank gun, on a mountainside near Anzio. Dan recalls his dad saying that he was "thrown downhill" when shrapnel struck the roof of his mouth and knocked out his teeth.

After spending four days in a field hospital, Raleigh rejoined his unit, which, later in 1944, shipped out to France.

On September 30 of that year, manning an outpost on a densely wooded hill there, he held off a squad of German attackers with grenades and rifle fire as a comrade trained a mortar on the enemy. For thirty minutes, the two Americans kept the advancing Germans at bay, as machine-gun bullets whizzed about them. The declaration awarding Raleigh a Silver Star for this "gallantry in action" said the Germans had crept within ten yards of the American position before Raleigh and his fellow GI drove them off.

Promoted in the field to buck sergeant, Raleigh was leading a charge near St. Die, France, when a German bullet pierced a lung. Dismayed that this wound signaled an end to his military service, he boarded the hospital ship *Algonquin* and headed for the Valley and home.

A new life awaited him, one framed by family—he would raise three sons—and a life dedicated to his community and, most of all, his fellow vets.

3

AIR CORPS AVIATORS

DUTCH EBERT: FIRST IN WAR

Perhaps the greatest unsung success story of AAF [Army Air Forces] training was navigators. The Army graduated some 50,000 during the war. And many had never flown out of sight of land before leaving "Uncle Sugar" for a war zone. Yet the huge majority found their way across oceans and continents without getting lost or running out of fuel—a stirring tribute to the AAF's educational establishments.
—Spitfire Association

His full handle is Harry Windsor Ebert Jr., but pretty much his entire life he's been known simply as "Dutch."

Now the Harry he knows full well about; that was his dad's name. Of the Windsor, he's unsure. But the "Dutch" is inexplicable.

Yes, the name *Ebert* does boast Germanic origins; in fact, it is said to be derived from the Old German word *Hildeberht*, meaning "battle-glorious," which in the context of this column is most fitting.

But the nickname, as Dutch told me last week, is usually pinned on a youngster with a distinct German accent, an obvious "Dutchman." And, thus, not on a boy who grew up on the corner of Cork and Stewart Streets and was born directly across East Piccadilly from the future site of the George Washington Hotel.

"Dutch" Ebert. *Courtesy of the Stewart Bell Jr. Archives, Winchester, Virginia.*

That latter tidbit tells you something. The GW went up in 1924, so that means Dutch must be in his nineties. He is, as he'll happily announce, precisely "ninety-six and three-fourths." He'll turn ninety-seven on May 20.

What Dutch will also tell an interested listener, though he has no surefire way of verifying it, is that he believes he was the first Winchester boy to see actual combat in World War II, at least in the European theater. Given that his first missions as a gunner/navigator aboard a B-24 predated Operation Torch, the Anglo-American invasion of North Africa, he may very well be right. But even if he's not, that's where our story begins.

A 1935 graduate of Handley, Dutch attended Randolph-Macon College in Ashland for three years before transferring to U. Va. to take business courses. He then worked for a year before deciding to enlist in the U.S. Army Air Forces. War, he believed, was imminent, and so he opted to join up early, in order to attend flight school.

War, in fact, did come soon enough. Dutch remembers marching to the mess hall during basic training in Montgomery, Alabama, when he heard the news of Japan's devastating attack on Pearl Harbor on December 7, 1941. "The only thing I thought about," he says, "was that I wouldn't be home for Christmas."

After basic, Dutch opted to enroll in the first specialty school available, which turned out to be for prospective navigators. For Dutch, an excellent math student, it proved a fortuitous choice. He not only finished at the head of his class at Turner Field in Albany, Georgia, but says he also helped two of his roommates successfully "navigate" the coursework.

Dutch's stellar work in the classroom earned for him an opportunity for assignment to a special task force of twenty-one B-24s, code-named HALPRO and commanded by Colonel Harry A. Halverson. Initially formed to attack Japan from airfields in China, the task force was redirected to the European theater when Rangoon fell and the Burma Road was cut, making logistical support of the detachment in China next to impossible.

That suited Dutch fine, as he considered any and all strikes against Japan in mid-1942, but especially in the wake of the Doolittle raid, to be "suicide missions."

And so, in the spring of that year, he and his mates left MacDill Field near Tampa, bound first for Brazil and then for Khartoum in the Anglo-Egyptian Sudan—where no official bases or ground crews awaited them.

DUTCH EBERT: TO PLOESTI AND BACK

Pat Boxwell of Handley Avenue was but a little girl, six or seven years old, when her older brother, Lieutenant Harry W. "Dutch" Ebert Jr., was learning the ways of the B-24 Liberator.

As Pat told me recently—actually at the latest Winchester Musica Viva concert, at which her daughter Laura and my wife, Toni, sang—she would send letters to Dutch featuring her handprint. He would reciprocate from whatever base or port of call he was stationed at.

In 1942, Pat was liable to get mail from just about anywhere—from Tampa to Khartoum to Fayid near the Suez Canal. Dutch got around that first full year of America's involvement in World War II.

In fact, when we left him last week, he and his small squadron of twenty-one B-24s—aka HALPRO (short for the Halverson project, so named for commanding officer Colonel Harry A Halverson)—were en route to Khartoum in the Anglo-Egyptian Sudan from MacDill Field near Tampa.

As Dutch, a navigator-gunner in this handpicked detachment, recalls, it was not an easy trip. Remember, these were the days before radio contact, so there was great reliance on basic instruments, particularly when flying through the series of thunderstorms that belabored this squadron as it made its way, first to Brazil and then to Africa.

"I know a continent [Africa] was there somewhere," Dutch said. "The sun came up, and I was able to get my bearings from the sun. I knew where I was." The trouble was, though, no ground crews awaited Dutch and his mates at Khartoum, and they ended up requisitioning British bases.

HALPRO's essential mission was lending assistance to the Royal Air Force not merely in protecting British supplies in North Africa but also in wreaking havoc on German lines servicing Field Marshal Erwin Rommel's Afrika Korps, which at that juncture was having its way with England's 8th Army. The decisive second Battle of El Alamein was still months in the distance.

But in June, HALPRO was dispatched far and wide on a historic mission. The United States had just expanded its declaration of war to include Romania, and so Dutch's crew and twelve others received orders to bomb the Ploesti oil fields, 30 miles from Bucharest—a 2,600-mile round trip made all the more difficult by a circuitous route around defiantly neutral Turkey.

Halverson, nicknamed "Hurry-Up Harry," produced a heavily creased *National Geographic* map that obscured the Turkish boundary. And so the B-24s, on June 12, took a slightly more direct route to the Black Sea, where they swung to the left and headed for Romania.

Dutch remembers getting within a short distance of the oil fields "when weather socked us in." By the time the skies cleared, they were over Bucharest, where Dutch's pilot spied a railyard. "He left it up to me whether to bomb it or not," Dutch says. "I thought, this is such a pretty city, so I found another target, a small refinery."

The B-24 dropped its payload and, dangerously low on fuel, headed back to its base at Fayid. Dutch recalls having three choices: refuel in Russia, cross neutral Turkey or stop at Aleppo in Syria. His pilot picked Aleppo, and the Liberator made it home "with 15 minutes of gas supply left."

This modest raid—not to be confused with the second, and more costly, attack on Ploesti a year later—marked the first U.S. airstrike on a European target.

Three days later, Dutch was back in the air, as HALPRO helped the RAF chase an Italian fleet sent to intercept a British convoy bound for the supply depot on Malta, back to its base at Taranto.

Forty-eighty hours later, in the June 17 *Evening Star*, sister Pat and the folks at home read this headline: "U.S. Bombers Score 35 Hits; Dutch Ebert Blasts Italians."

DUTCH IN THE DESERT

On the morning of November 15, 1942, Lieutenant Harry W. "Dutch" Ebert Jr. and his crew climbed into their B-24 Liberator and headed west from Egypt across North Africa. Their target: German installations near the Libyan city of Tripoli.

They would return. Their plane would not. It was the only time Dutch (Handley class of 1935) recalls being "scared"—"really scared"—while serving as navigator/gunner aboard his workhorse B-24. He had good reason.

The weather was perfect during the five-hour flight until his squadron came within forty miles of its destination. A rolling series of storms "socked us in," he says.

One of the flight leaders, a West Point grad Dutch remembers as "a pain in the neck," said the crews could ditch their bombs in the Mediterranean and head for home. All did but Dutch's, which decided to strike a German supply dump near Benghazi.

His B-24 peeled off from the loose formation, delivered its payload and turned for Egypt. He and his mates were seventy miles south of the Mediterranean when five fighters—ME-109s, Messerschmitts—burst from the clouds. Dutch had heard of the fabled German aircraft but had never seen one—until those five had his lone-flying Liberator in their sights.

The first attack, he recalls, knocked out one of the B-24's four engines and badly damaged the propeller on another. A second attack got another engine, and with the plane gradually losing altitude, Dutch could sense "we were going down." And he knew, simply knew, the Germans would circle around and attack a third time. "One more attack would have finished us," he says.

But whether due to a shortage of ammunition or of fuel, this third strike never came. The Liberator, though, was still in trouble and losing altitude faster.

If not for their injured tail-gunner, wounded in the shoulder and neck, Dutch and his crew could have bailed out. But they wouldn't leave their comrade to die. So they crash-landed the plane in the desert with its wheels up—on terrain resembling, Dutch says, that of Arizona or New Mexico. Enveloped in a cloud of dust, the plane, when viewed for a moment through the setting sun, "looked like it was on fire," he adds.

Fortunately, a British fighter spotted them, and the pilot tipped his wings. Now it was a question of who would arrive first to the crash site—a British ground crew or a German patrol. It proved to be the former. The British picked up the crew the following morning and quickly initiated them into the Late Arrivals Club, whose motto was "Never Too Late to Come Back."

For the record, the tail-gunner survived. Years later, Dutch looked him up in New York but abandoned his search when the phone book boasted "ninety-three people with the same name."

Upon returning to their base, Dutch and his crew spent three days of R&R (rest and rehabilitation) in Tel Aviv and then were called back into action—though not for long. They had completed their requisite forty bombing missions, which earned them a ticket home—and, for Dutch, a new billet as a flight instructor.

He asked to be stationed east of the Mississippi, but in true military fashion, the army sent him to Tucson. Fate, though, had intervened fortuitously. Not only was the weather fine, but while there he also met his future wife, Carol, a New York City girl who had gone west, to the University of Arizona, for her education and, she admits, a "good time." They married in 1945.

Duly discharged, Dutch brought Carol back to Winchester, where he took over his dad's Buick dealership on North Loudoun. He sold the business in 1973 and retired shortly thereafter.

From World War II, Dutch, now ninety-six, still has his medals—a Silver Star and a Distinguished Flying Cross—and a pair of flying gloves, which look as good as new.

John Ecelberger: God Works in Mysterious Ways

Jean Ecelberger firmly adheres to the notion that "God works in mysterious ways." After all, she says, her husband's life, particularly his wartime experiences, testified to that adage.

Phillip O. Ecelberger—Pennsylvania born and bred but a resident of Frederick County at the time of his death earlier this year—was a combat photographer and developer assigned to the IX Troop Carrier Command during World War II.

That Ecelberger was even assigned such duties is the stuff of serendipity. He became a witness to history, to some of the landmark events of our time, by accident. Or maybe through good fortune. Or, as his wife of sixty-two years says, by Providence working "mysteriously."

Call it what you will, but nothing, most likely, seemed divinely inspired at the time, at least not for a lad of twenty-one "young and anxious to do what all men want to do." Ecelberger's path to that photographer's billet was serpentine, and his first weeks in the service of Uncle Sam were frustrating, Jean says. It all started the day he tried to join the war effort.

Ecelberger intended to enlist with his brother Dick and his cousin Byron Sheesley in August 1942. But an inability to locate his birth certificate in his hometown of Big Run, Pennsylvania, stalled the process. A new one had to be made, delaying his entry to active duty until September 7.

After going through basic training in the U.S. Army Air Corps, Ecelberger was ready to ship out with his unit when he encountered another bend in the road. He contracted the measles.

From there, Jean says, "he almost got lost," but a general "found" Ecelberger and befriended him, to the point that, if he wanted to, he could have remained stateside for the duration of hostilities. "But he wanted to go," Jean says, "and the general saw to it that he did. But he did not go with his [original] unit."

A childhood interest in photography prompted Private Ecelberger, then stationed at Lowry Field in Denver, to enroll in the photography course at the Air Forces Technical School on base. He graduated and, on October 21, 1943, boarded a ship for Scotland and the massive armed camp that was the British Isles.

"He went to photography school as a result of not shipping out," Jean says. "He was disappointed at not shipping out....He wanted to go....That's what I mean when I say God works in mysterious ways."

The IX Troop Carrier Command came into being as an arm of the 9th Air Force five days before Ecelberger set sail for Scotland. Its mission was to provide air transport for the soon-to-be-famous Allied airborne divisions, then training for the invasion of Hitler's Fortress Europe.

In time, the IX's C-47 Skytrain aircraft would ferry men and supplies and tow the fabled Horsa gliders to the skies over Normandy in the early hours of D-Day, June 6, 1944.

Later, the IX performed the same transport duties over Holland during the ill-fated Operation Market Garden (September 17–25, 1944) and finally over the Rhine during the final push on Germany (March 1945). Between these two operations, in late December 1944, the aviators flew critical supplies to the embattled men of the 101st Airborne, huddled in the besieged Belgian town of Bastogne during the Battle of the Bulge.

Ecelberger, attached to the carrier command's headquarters, had earned his sergeant's stripes and was in charge of a thirteen-man photography lab. Though reluctant in later years to talk at length about his accomplishments, he was awarded a Bronze Star, Jean says, for "improving the process to print photos faster." As his discharge papers indicate, his labors also included developing aerial photos for use as maps.

Ecelberger also took his share of combat shots. Jean remembers him relating trips aboard the Horsa gliders, an experience he termed "quite thrilling." He also had a bit of the daredevil in him, setting his five-foot, seven-inch frame as far as possible "on the outside of a plane with a camera" in hand.

Though they attended different high schools, Phil and Jean Ecelberger were childhood sweethearts. They met in Sunday school.

A farm boy, Ecelberger grew up outside the Jefferson County town of Big Run in the west-central part of Pennsylvania. Jean (an abbreviation of her given name, Geneva) hailed from Sykesville, about thirty miles to the northeast, but she moved to Jefferson when her father, formerly the operator of a company store, bought a farm adjoining the Ecelberger spread.

Ecelberger graduated from Big Run High in June 1941. Jean, three years his junior, received her diploma from Punxsutawney High in the town known for its Groundhog Day celebration.

Somehow, in those latter days of the Depression, Jean recalls, Ecelberger was able to find work as an office boy at U.S. Steel in Youngstown, Ohio. His connection to Youngstown was his cousin Byron, who often spent the summer in Big Run. When the time came, Ecelberger and his brother Dick returned the favor, heading west to seek employment.

It was in Ohio, at Fort Hayes, that Phil was inducted into the military. And, in 1945, it was to Youngstown—and U.S. Steel—not Big Run, that Ecelberger eventually returned after the war.

He and Jean resumed their romance and were married the following year. "We figured we had to get to know each other again," Jean says.

Ecelberger worked in the chemical lab, running tests on metals, at the "Ohio works" brought to life in the Bruce Springsteen song "Youngstown" until U.S. Steel opened its sprawling Fairless manufacturing compound outside Philadelphia in the 1950s. He got in, Jean says, on the "ground floor" at Fairless, eventually retiring as chief chemist.

During those years, the Ecelbergers raised three children, all of whom now reside in the Old Dominion. Katie Eplett, an assistant manager at Talbot's at the Pentagon City mall, and Brenda Mallinak, a tax attorney in Vienna, live in Northern Virginia. A third daughter, Lucinda Thomas, a part-time reference librarian at Shenandoah University, calls the Canterburg community south of Stephens City home.

It was during a trip to visit Lucinda, or Cindy, then living in Edinburg, that Jean fell in love with the Shenandoah Valley. She wanted to move here. Ecelberger was less enthusiastic. "He dragged his feet," Jean says. "We were living in Bucks County, [Pennsylvania] in a big house."

Still, Jean ultimately carried the day on that decision and, some fifteen years ago, the Ecelbergers packed up that "big house" and moved to The Summit in northern Frederick County. And with them came albums of old photos from a distant era that, for years, had sat on a shelf in a Bucks County garage collecting dust.

Phil Ecelberger was, by nature, "a very quiet individual," his widow says. "He never talked much about himself. Most people did not get to know him." So, while Jean knew full well that he had brought that treasure trove of photographic memories home from the service—some of them still with the government's "Censored" stamp on the back—she never did learn which of the photos he actually took and which he merely developed and printed. "He didn't talk about it enough for me to know how much he did and didn't do," Jean says.

Upon examination, it does seem clear that some of the snaps in Ecelberger's collection were taken "officially." Others merely record the day-to-day existence of young men at war. All speak to a day, a time and the accomplishments—at once prosaic and monumental—of a generation this nation proudly calls its "greatest."

The pictures would emerge from time to time, to be displayed at reunions of Phil's unit. But there were moments, Jean remembers, when Ecelberger "used to say he'd just throw them away."

"I'd say, 'Phillip, no,' and the girls would say the same thing," Jean says. "He could still look at the pictures and know and could tell you just what was going on."

About five or six years ago, Jean adds, officials at the George C. Marshall Museum and Research Library, located on the parade ground of the Virginia Military Institute in Lexington, got wind of the photos and asked to see them.

Ecelberger took them the original albums, which were accepted as a donation to the museum's substantial collection of World War II papers, photographs and memorabilia. Jean now has a CD on which all the photos—her husband's life and times in the army—are stored.

If anything, Jean says, Ecelberger never lamented donating the photos, essentially to posterity. What did "upset" him, though, nearly from the moment he mustered out of service, was that the army confiscated the cameras his unit used during the war. Though bulky, the model featured what Jean calls a "fixed focus," which allowed Ecelberger and his wartime photographers the latter-day luxury of pointing and shooting. An aerial view of Paris and the Arc de Triomphe, in which people, though small, are clearly visible on the ground, attests to the camera's capabilities.

After the war came to a close in Europe, Ecelberger and his crew were told they were headed for the Pacific. So all their equipment was stowed away. But, before the unit could transition to a new theater of operations, the atom bombs were dropped on Hiroshima and Nagasaki, compelling Japan to surrender.

As Ecelberger would later learn, the technology he treasured was confiscated by the military and subsequently burned. "That was his biggest lament," Jean says. "No matter how much I paid for a camera for him after that, he was never satisfied."

Settling in The Summit, Phil and Jean Ecelberger enjoyed a vigorous retirement. He played golf. She gardened, and he aided in that endeavor. They were active in a drive to plant trees in the development ringing Lake Holiday. They enjoyed the occasional game of bridge.

But when Ecelberger's health began to deteriorate, Jean felt they needed to be even closer to family. So they bought a four-acre lot just a stone's throw from daughter Cindy's home on Double Church Road south of Stephens City and built a comfortable and handicapped-accessible, one-story house. They resided there about three years.

This past January 15, Phil died at the age of eighty-seven. "It's just beginning to hit me," Jean says. "I've been to a few funerals lately." It's also given her time to reflect—about their life together and the war that shaped them both, and an entire generation. "It was a different war," she says, "a war that the whole community, the whole nation was behind."

And when it was over, the men left the tools of war behind, came home and moved on with their lives, often with significant success.

Cousin Byron Sheesley, a pilot who flew over Europe, became a well-respected surgeon. Brother Dick Ecelberger, a paratrooper with the renowned 101st Airborne, went to work delivering fuel for a home heating-oil company. He ended up owning the firm. And Phil rose through the ranks of U.S. Steel to become chief chemist at the Fairless Works.

"These fellows went into service from Depression families," Jean says, "and look what they did with their lives."

And how would Phil feel at the prospect of his last "hometown" newspaper publishing those photos that he kept stored on a shelf in his Bucks County garage?

"Oh," Jean says, "he would have been so, so proud."

4

CARMEL WHETZEL

Daring POW

Carmel Whetzel can't recall how he and two of his barracks-mates got their hands on some wire cutters—only that they did. And one night in late March 1945, this essential tool of the prison-break trade performed admirably when the West Virginia–born Whetzel, now eighty-seven and residing in Winchester, and his two buddies busted out of a German POW compound and roamed the Mecklenburg countryside for two weeks.

In the two decades immediately following World War II, prison-camp movies were Hollywood staples. *Stalag 17* and *The Great Escape* spring quickly to mind, as does *The Bridge on the River Kwai*. Sixties-era TV even boasted a spoof of the genre, the long-running series *Hogan's Heroes*.

As art can—and often does—imitate life, Whetzel could have been a technical adviser for any of these efforts, whether "silver" or small screen. For not only did he live the life of a POW, but also, somehow, lived to talk about it.

But that's getting a bit ahead of the story.

FROM LOST RIVER TO FRANCE

Born and raised on a hilltop farm overlooking Lost River State Park near Mathias, West Virginia, Carmel B. Whetzel, one of ten children, "ran away from home" when he was sixteen. Landing in Baltimore County, Maryland, he worked at a hog farm, then for a tire company and finally for Maryland Drydock and Shipyard Company.

World War II intervened and, at age nineteen, Whetzel received the inevitable call from Uncle Sam. September 7, 1944, found him and the rest of his mates in Company M, 3rd Battalion, 104th Infantry Regiment, 26th Infantry Division, disembarking at Cherbourg, France.

For the better part of the next two months, Whetzel piloted trucks for the famed Red Ball Express, ferrying sorely needed fuel, supplies and food to the soldiers on the front lines. He also drove a jeep.

On November 2, 1944, elements of the 3rd Battalion "pushed ahead" to the French town of Rodalbe in the province of Lorraine.

Carmel Whetzel. *Courtesy of Carmel Whetzel.*

German troops surrounded the Americans, killing many and seizing about two hundred as prisoners of war.

Whetzel and two other drivers evaded capture by running into a barn and diving beneath a "haymow."

Captured

For three days, Whetzel and his comrades dared not move from their place of hiding—even as German soldiers took turns sleeping on piles of straw directly above them. Only when they heard the telltale fire of American guns did they reveal themselves.

But it was not Americans coming to their rescue who were discharging the guns, but rather Germans firing captured weaponry. Whetzel and his friends walked out of their hiding place into German hands.

Taken initially to Stalag 12A near Limburg, Germany, Whetzel did not eat for a week but was forced to peel potatoes for his German captors. "We couldn't eat," he says, "and, if we tried, a guard would hit you over the head with a rifle butt."

He and his fellow POWs were stripped of their GI uniforms and given raggedy old clothes and wooden shoes. Their uniforms, as they later learned, were used by German infiltrators posing as American MPs during the Battle of the Bulge.

Ten days before Christmas, Whetzel boarded a 40x8 railroad car (so-called because it could hold either eight horses or forty men) for his transfer to Stalag 2A near Neubrandenburg, north of Berlin.

This stalag had roughly fifty ancillary camps, known as Arbeitskommando, where POWs were subjected to hard labor seven days a week. Whetzel was dispatched to one such camp, located at a Luftwaffe base near Parchim, where he caught a glimpse of Germany's prototypical jet fighters sitting on the runway.

At Parchim, a captured French priest provided a fellow POW, Albert J. "Steve" Stevens, enough paper to keep a diary and, more important, to record the names and home addresses of all the men in the contingent. On pages sixty and sixty-one of the diary are recorded the events of March 26, 1945.

Escape...to Nowhere

Wire cutters duly procured, Whetzel and his two bunkies, Harvey "Ikie" Boulerice and Roy Miller, hatched their plan for escape.

They knew each night a guard would pass through and check each individual room in the barracks. On the night in question, the threesome saw the guard start his rounds and then moved to the room closest to the front door—which they found unlocked.

They slipped out of the barracks and into the latrine out back.

"We went through the cr—er hole and cut the fence and crawled through," he says. "The guards didn't stop us. I don't know if they even saw us. We didn't care. We just walked down the road."

And kept walking. For two weeks, they lived off the land—relieving chicken coops of their inhabitants to sustain themselves—until a German "forest guard" spotted them and picked them up.

Whetzel says the trio would have gone farther afield had it not been for their inability to ford swollen canals. When they returned to camp, they were carrying a chicken.

"Day of Days"

Summarily put on trial, Whetzel and his fellow escapees were not sentenced to death—as may have been the case earlier in the war—but to three weeks of confinement with a diet of bread and water. They were housed in a compound reserved for Russian prisoners.

Though Allied forces were inching closer as winter turned fully to spring in 1945, the work did not stop. When American warplanes blew up a railroad, Whetzel and the POWs were sent to repair it.

One day, they saw a U.S. plane shot down. On another, seven POWs fell victim to friendly fire when U.S. aircraft strafed the area in which they were working. Whetzel and the other prisoners dug a trench and buried their buddies.

On May 2 came the "day of days," as Stevens wrote in the diary. The war was over, at least in that sector. Oddly enough, after detonating all available ammunition, the guards herded the prisoners to a wooded area—and then departed.

For about six hours, the men huddled together, wondering what to do. Eventually, they decided to march back to their compound, where Russian troops liberated them two days later.

Back Home

Carmel Whetzel returned home to Baltimore, to a lifetime of hard work—in many vocations and avocations.

True to his Red Ball roots, he drove a tractor-trailer for Amoco for thirty-three years and served as his union's shop steward for twenty-eight of those. In 1969, he mixed race-car fuel for three events at the "Brickyard," Indianapolis Motor Speedway.

He also "moonlighted" as a painter and learned the cabinetmaking trade, eventually setting up his own shop to toil in those "off" hours when he wasn't driving for Amoco.

In later years, after taking early retirement, Whetzel and his son started building homes and townhouses in the Baltimore area and in Ocean City, Maryland. "I'm just a hillbilly," he says. "Never got in trouble...but I have worked seven days a week all my life."

Not until his mid-seventies, though, did Whetzel, still lean as a greyhound, begin to look back and reconnect with those men with whom he had formed everlasting bonds during the crucible of war.

Oddly enough, it all started when he decided to purchase POW tags for his automobile. He then joined a POW club and, in 2009, attended his first POW/MIA Recognition Day in Andersonville, Georgia, where he was presented a certificate signed by former Virginia governor Tim Kaine.

This past September, Whetzel returned to Andersonville under the sponsorship of Rolling Thunder, the biker organization dedicated to the heightened appreciation of veterans.

Three years ago, Whetzel moved to Winchester to be closer to the Veterans Administration hospital in Martinsburg, West Virginia. He and his third wife, Carol—Whetzel's first two wives, Mary Jo (mother of his five children) and Dorothy, have predeceased him—reside on Harvest Ridge Drive.

Outside their home, two flags fly daily. One is Old Glory; the other—fittingly—is the American Ex-Prisoners of War flag.

5

"THE BULGE"

BILL BUTLER: "WAR IS HELL"

There's no limit to human endurance.
—Favorite saying of H.W. "Bill" Butler Jr.

Extremities, digits, hands and feet — or, more precisely, fingers and toes. For Harry William Butler Jr.—serial number 33-539-939—these appendages, frostbitten nearly sixty-six years ago, are a daily reminder of his military service in the Second World War. For Butler, eighty-six, now residing with his daughter Liz in Sunnyside, such is the legacy of an Ardennes winter. And of a tumultuous, complex and thoroughly confusing (particularly for those actively involved) battle known simply as "The Bulge," Germany's last-ditch lightning thrust to unlock victory from the grip of defeat just before Christmas in 1944. "There are days I can't straighten my hands," Butler says, his keen and active mind reeling in recollections of the coldest European winter in decades. "It looks like I have claws." But then, unlike so many of a generation given to reticence, Bill Butler has seldom, if ever, shied away from memory. Truth be told, he has embraced it.

"The movie *Saving Private Ryan* cracked the egg on remembrance for so many veterans," says his son H.W. Butler III, still known as "Spunky." "But Dad was never that inward."

And, by virtue of positions held—VFW post commander, longtime state chairman of the Veterans Council—he was often very outward in holding veterans' affairs to the light. He was, for example, a driving force in raising $45,000 for a permanent veterans' memorial and meeting place in Shenandoah Memorial Park. "I grew tired of being downtown, in front of the courthouse, with no one there on Veterans Day," he says, noting the impetus for the erection of the memorial. And when it was built, the man hailed locally as "Mr. VFW" made certain that nary a Veterans Day or Memorial Day passed without proper remembrance, pomp and ceremony. Such devotion did not go unnoticed. In 2003, a grateful city proclaimed November 11—Veterans Day—as H.W. "Bill" Butler Day in Winchester. "My dad is one of Winchester's most decorated vets," Spunky says, simply and proudly. And his is an amazing story.

Everyone asked me why I wasn't serving.
—Bill Butler

Some men are eager warriors, others are reluctant warriors. Bill Butler was, if anything, a conscientious warrior. Born in 1924, Butler was a senior at Handley High School when Japan attacked Pearl Harbor in December 1941. The next fall, he matriculated at Virginia Tech. America was fully at war when Butler came home for Christmas in 1942, and he quickly wearied of penetrating stares and of the inevitable statement followed by a question: "My son's at war. Why aren't you?"

Bill Butler. *Courtesy of the Stewart Bell Jr. Archives, Winchester, Virginia.*

So, along with his Handley buddy and Tech classmate Robert "Snuffy" Taylor, Butler decided to enlist. He wanted to join the infantry but was assigned to the U.S. Army Air Corps. Snuffy desired the air corps but got the infantry.

Butler spent twenty months in the U.S. Air Corps, which included basic training in Miami Beach, where he and his colleagues incurred the wrath of residents with their nonstop rendition of the corps song as they practiced close-order drills on a local golf course. Butler may have remained stateside, in an air corps training unit, for the duration of the war had it not been for his still-burning desire to join the infantry. One day, while stationed at MacDill Field in Tampa, he spotted a bulletin requesting noncommissioned officers—he was then a corporal—to volunteer for the infantry. Though his commanding officer considered him "crazy," Butler jumped at the opportunity.

And, come the late days of autumn in 1944, he was wading ashore in France as a newly minted sergeant in the Ammunition & Pioneer Platoon, Headquarters Company, 1st Battalion, 424th Infantry Regiment, 106th Infantry Division. The 106th had been dispatched in relief of the 2nd Infantry Division. The morning of December 16 found Butler and his men comfortably billeted at a home on a ridge near the village of Steinebruck on the German side of the Oure River that separates that country from Belgium. Their duffel bags had yet to arrive, and they had just started unloading their combat gear, when all hell broke loose. "I started the day in Germany and ended the day in Belgium." For the men who bore the initial brunt of Germany's last great offensive, the opening hours of "The Bulge"—so-called for the huge dent it created in the Allied lines—are, to this day, miasma, chaos, confusion.

There was "no military information," Butler recalls, and "no organized resistance." And very little ammunition. As reserve troops stationed in a supposedly "quiet" sector, he and his men carried but forty rifle rounds per man. Complicating the situation was the presence of English-speaking Germans disguised as American MPs, who wrought logistical havoc by switching road signs and providing wrong directions. Later, Butler and his fellow GIs would learn that the Germans also executed prisoners of war, most notably in what became known as the "Malmedy Massacre." "Malmedy went through our lines like wildfire," Butler says. "After Malmedy got out, we showed no mercy. And, after the infiltration of our lines [by the English-speaking Germans], if you didn't know the right password, you were shot."

Desperate times, desperate measures—and those first forty-eight hours of The Bulge were desperate, as German tanks and infantry poured into the Ardennes Forest. The 424th's two sister regiments, the 422nd and 423rd, deployed at the point of the German attack, were cut off and surrounded—and ultimately surrendered, earning the dubious distinction of being "the first American troops to cross the Rhine."

Butler and his men, deployed farther to the south, escaped such a fate in what he describes as "highly confused war." In the battle's early stages, he recalled in the August 1990 edition of *The Bulge Bugle*, "We moved around a lot. We would make a stand here and there as we had no organized resistance larger than a platoon. Everyone had their own little war going on." For Butler, this entailed a lifetime's worth of hair-raising experiences in a time frame of mere hours. He remembers crawling among the tombstones of a churchyard—thinking ever so much of a German soldier doing likewise in the World War I film *All Quiet on the Western Front*—as the sky rained artillery shells. Moments later, a mortar shell whizzed past his head—too close, in truth, for the shrapnel to get him, and so close for the concussion to burn his eyes and hurt his eardrums. He woke up on the floor of the church. Butler escaped the onrushing Germans when he managed to reach the bed of a small trailer pulled by a jeep, whose driver sped away just ahead of the Wehrmacht advance. And finally, sometime later that day, Butler somehow avoided capture when German troops rushed through a barn in which he was lying, his eyes still bandaged from the wound he received from the mortar round. "Someone whom I never saw" relieved him of his watch—a treasure he had purchased with money earned working for his father—but not his life.

"I stole one back off a German," he says, "as soon as I got the chance." Eventually, Butler and a small cadre of soldiers, roughly sixty-five in all, scrambled back to the Belgian town of St. Vith, site of the 106th's headquarters, where they "were welcomed with open arms" as men "who had already been written off the books." It was there that Butler, still but a lad of twenty, received an order he has never forgotten—an order that made him realize that "infantry is expendable."

"We were told to hold the line for three days and, if necessary, to die there," he says. "That kind of scared me." Assigned to dig in at a bridge at the town's crossroads, Butler occupied what he calls "the single [fox]hole of St. Vith." "No one around commanded me, and I commanded the foxhole for myself," he says. Butler and the rest of the beleaguered defenders of St. Vith hung on until the 82nd Airborne Division launched a counterattack so that the remnants of the 106th could retreat from the collapsing pocket surrounding the town.

Sgt. Butler…performed meritorious service in combat
from 21 to 24 December 1944.
—Bronze Star citation

Falling back to the village of Bracht, Butler and his company dug in anew. But the relentless German advance denied them any comfort. With the enemy threatening to turn his battalion's flank, Butler, trained only in the use of the M-1 rifle, turned himself into a machine-gunner, "learning as he fired." As the citation quoted above notes, he also "openly risked his life" canvassing the area for ammunition. With nerves at a breaking point and men abandoning their positions as the Germans pushed forward, Butler endeavored to rally his unit and, at the same time, maintain a measure of resistance to slow the enemy horde. His example "inspired" his comrades back to the cause at hand.

"For three days," the citation reads, "he effectively used the machine gun protecting the left flank and, by his alertness, aided greatly in holding the enemy off." The next day was Christmas, and a letter written home suggests that the events of the previous week had yet to truly sink in. In a few understated lines to his parents, hurriedly dashed off, Butler said, "Going has been a little tough lately, but I for one personally am in one piece and fairly well off. Nothing to brag about, but I thank God I came through OK." But, years later in *The Bulge Bugle* he would observe, "I had no one to wish me a Merry Christmas even if I had known what day it was. Christmas had come and gone. There were no decorations or Christmas carols, but the Ardennes Forest was full of Christmas trees covered with snow." "War was hell. It wasn't fun—soggy feet and cold."

By the time New Year's Day 1945 rolled around, the tide of the battle was turning. General George Patton and his 3rd Army, for instance, had rushed to the aid of the encircled town of Bastogne, roughly twenty-five miles southwest of St. Vith. For Bill Butler, though, the tumult of the previous two weeks had taken its toll. He had not bathed since November 21 and had scarcely had time enough to sleep peacefully since December 15. And his feet were killing him. But he was off the front line.

On New Year's Eve, he wrote to his father, saying, "Well, at least, I'm out of the fight for a while. We are back of the lines for a rest…after hell on earth. Here we are in a house in Belgium and it has a radio in it. Good ol' American news and broadcasts of music….Had a small dose of frostbite and trench foot, but the shells cured all my minor pains with fright. I'm carrying on." But two mornings later, Butler awakened with "the shakes" and feeling "paralyzed." The diagnosis: combat fatigue and frostbite—or, as he says, "just worn out."

After four days of what can only be called "heroic treatment"—exposure of his hands and feet in a makeshift hospital that was itself freezing cold—he returned to his unit. Today, he says that he did so largely to escape further "treatment," which might have included amputation. By January 18, Butler could write to his father that "I believe that I have hardened to the war now and the cold snowy weather is feeling better so I believe I'm a man now whether you disagree or not."

Two days later, the 106th returned to the front in time to participate in the recapture of St. Vith. Butler and his men "ended up only 500 yards [from] where we had started" on December 16. Then the long slog toward and into Germany began. Action was, Butler says, "constant but inconclusive"—nothing to rival the last two weeks of December—and in early March, after eighty-one days of nonstop combat, the division stopped at the banks of the Rhine and moved out of the battle zone. Back to France for rest, rehabilitation—and a long-awaited bath. Bill Butler was finally able to shed a tattered air corps shirt he had worn beneath his uniform the entire campaign. Still, as an E-8 (technical sergeant)—or, as he says, "the sergeant in charge"—he could not bathe until all his men had done so.

Nonetheless, those days when "you could smell yourself climbing into bed" were over.

"THE PRIZE CATCH OF BERRYVILLE"

I showed him my medals; he wanted a commission.
—Bill Butler

Bill Butler was back on the Rhine—in a pup tent, he says—when the war in Europe ended in May 1945.

Like many soldiers in that theater, he awaited news of a possible redeployment to the Pacific. But, in the wake of atomic bombs dropped on the Japanese cities of Hiroshima and Nagasaki, the war ended as Butler was in transit from Europe to America.

There would be no reassignment, and so, on Labor Day 1945, he walked through the door of his parents' home on Clifford Street. His father was reading the newspaper.

Butler recalls their exchange as if it happened yesterday. Pretty much the first words out of H.W. Sr.'s mouth were, "Well, you never made lieutenant." Bill responded by showing his dad his medals. The elder Butler's response was the same.

Why was this an issue? Because H.W. Sr., a machine-gunner in the First World War, had received a commission in 1923. And Bill's older brother Joe, a graduate of Virginia Tech, had received one, too, by dint of his membership in the school's cadet corps. Joe went on to serve in the Pacific in a support, rather than combat, capacity.

"There was a bit of sibling rivalry there," says son Spunky, "but it was also an enlisted man versus officer thing. Dad was proud to be a non-com."

Fortunately, that lack of an officer's bars did not keep H.W. Sr. from giving Bill a job (running one of his orchards) or a decent salary ($150 a month, as compared to his $128 a month army pay), or a car, or the offer of a house when he married.

But money to return to Tech? No way. "Not if you want all the things I'm giving you," Bill remembers his father saying.

So Bill ended up attending a number of colleges—Shepherd and Shenandoah, among them—but never earned a degree.

Nonetheless, he did quite well for himself as "a broker, exporter, packer, and shipper of Virginia apples." Enough to amply provide for two children—Spunky and Liz—the fruit of his union with a dazzling, dark-haired beauty who referred to herself as "the prize catch of Berryville."

"She said, 'Marry me now'—and we've been married ever since."

Rose Ellen Ramsburg, the youngest of seven children, met Bill Butler at York's Inn, a popular teenage gathering spot in Winchester, when they were still in high school.

Family lore, as Spunky tells it, suggests that the couple were "tight" before the war, but the relationship had its ups and downs, as adolescent romances frequently do.

Still, Rose Ellen, now eighty-five and residing in an extended-care facility in Front Royal, must have occupied a special place in Bill's heart, as he had carved her name into the stock of his M-1 rifle. And a Ramsburg family photo, taken in 1943, features Bill prominently.

But, to hear Bill relate the story, landing Rose Ellen was all about timing, about him getting home from the war earlier than her other potential suitors. "She had written to several guys during the war, and I think she wrote the same letter to all the guys," he says with just a hint of a grin. "And I had written to a few girls. Finally, I took my turn with her and she said, 'Marry me now'—and we've been married ever since."

How quickly were these wheels set in motion? Bill returned from service on Labor Day 1945. They married on October 22.

As a kid, you see the glory, like when you're playing with souvenirs—German Lugers, for example—brought home from the war. But as you grow older, and having been in the army myself, you realize it's just nice to be alive.
—Spunky Butler

As a boy growing up in postwar Winchester, Spunky Butler knew little, really, about the men who populated the main-traveled roads of his young life. And understandably so.

Miff Clowe was his father's friend, the mayor, not the National Guard officer who led his friends ashore on D-Day. Dutch Ebert was a car salesman, not a gunner-navigator on a B-24 Liberator.

Not until his adult years did Spunky truly appreciate these men for the roles they played in the war, for the gallantry and courage they displayed. But Bill—decorated veteran, apple broker and longtime city councilman—was a different story altogether. "Above all, he was my father," he says, "the authority figure, the guy I wanted to be proud of me. Him being who he is was one of the factors that drove me to VMI [Virginia Military Institute]."

Five days after graduating from VMI in 1969, at the height of the Vietnam War, Spunky went on active duty in the artillery. "I wanted something I could ride," he says. And his older son H.W. IV, born in 1972, served in the tank corps during peacetime.

Together, the three generations of Harry, along with Spunky's younger son, Morgan, returned to the Ardennes in 2000 to retrace Bill's footsteps in the snows of 1944.

They walked through the churchyard where Bill had crawled just prior to getting blinded by the mortar blast. They visited the field near Malmedy where the "massacre" of the American POWs had taken place. And, thanks to Morgan's ease with the French language, they gathered in "roundtable discussions" with grateful Belgiques eager to listen to an aging warrior speak of days gone by.

It was the trip of a lifetime. Ten years later, in March 2010, Bill took a much shorter journey—to the French embassy in Washington—to receive similar thanks from a much higher power. Namely, the French government, which ushered him and twenty-two other American World War II vets into the Legion of Honor. Bill, though ailing, managed to do something no other veteran could—appear in his old dress uniform.

You see, the spirit remains ever willing and the memories as vivid as the day they were created. "It was cold as hell over there, buddy," he'll tell you.

Something those digits—finger and toes—tell him most every day…about the absence of limits to human endurance.

Fred Gordon's Christmas

*What's merry about all this, you ask? We're fighting—it's cold—
we aren't home. All true, but what has the proud Eagle Division
accomplished...? Just this: We have stopped cold everything that
has been thrown at us from the north, east, southwest.*
—Brigadier General Anthony McAuliffe, Acting Commander,
101st Airborne Division, Christmas Eve 1944

You don't realize how cold it was.
—Fred Gordon, December 22, 2004

Fred Gordon once spent Christmas outdoors, in a foxhole, in what was called "the hole in the doughnut." The place was Bastogne, Belgium. The year was 1944.

Two weeks ago on the *Star*'s editorial page, I wrote a tribute to the men of the 101st Airborne Division, "The Screaming Eagles," who by chance and great fortune bore the brunt of Germany's blood and iron in what is known as "The Battle of the Bulge." Little did I realize that, in this little crossroads community on US 522 North, one of these heroic "Eagles" still lives—eighty-five-year-old Fred Gordon.

In the coming weeks along Valley Pike, you'll get to know Fred a little better. For now, allow me to place him where he was exactly sixty years ago—in the "hole" (or hell-hole) of that "doughnut."

The preceding six months had been busy for Fred. A machine-gunner and armorer in the 101st's 377th Parachute Field Artillery Battalion, he had jumped into France on D-Day and then participated in the ill-fated airborne attack on Holland—Operation Market Garden—later that autumn.

In fact, he and the other members of his unit had just returned to France from Holland when the urgent call came in mid-December: The 101st was needed in Belgium, in the Ardennes Forest, where the Germans had just attacked in force against lightly held positions, creating what would forever be called "The Bulge."

Fred Gordon. *Courtesy of the Stewart Bell Jr. Archives, Winchester, Virginia.*

Fred recalls the mad scramble for supplies as the division, on less than twelve hours' notice, received its orders to move by truck convoy. "We didn't know where we were going," he says.

They soon found out.

Their destination was the strategic town of Bastogne, where seven major roads and three railroads intersected. The Germans desperately wanted the town to maintain their advance; the Americans, just as desperately, needed to hold it. Christmas—and the snows of the coldest European winter in decades—was coming.

When Fred and his comrades arrived, it was raining. The precipitation soon turned to snow as Fred began to fashion his foxhole. Not on the front line, he was able to constantly improve his protective earthwork until it was a good three to four feet deep.

Fred doesn't remember much from that Christmas Day save for the bitter cold—"the trees were just as white as Santa Claus' beard"—and the fact that the Germans, who had the 101st completely surrounded, continually tried "to blow up the center of that doughnut."

"Those artillery shells," he says, "I didn't think they could get one in a foxhole. When they started getting close, I said, 'I believe maybe they can.'"

That never happened, of course, though Fred's best friend—"a rough guy but nice ol' fella from Ohio" named Moe Sowers—was killed when a shell landed near his unit's mess hall.

Poor visibility kept Allied aircraft grounded with needed supplies for Fred and the other besieged defenders. Ammunition was running so low, Fred says, that the 101st was under orders not to fire "unless you saw the whites of the Germans' eyes."

But the division grimly hung on and, in time, as the thrice-told tale of heroism goes, the C-47s finally flew and the 4th Armored Division of General George Patton's 3rd Army raced to the relief of the "battered bastion."

Fred remembers flak hitting the engine of one such supply plane a few days after Christmas. The C-47 went down right in front of him. Miraculously, the entire crew survived.

The division's inspired defense saved Bastogne and turned the tide of the huge land battle. But for years, Fred, though a proud veteran, did not dwell much on The Bulge or his role in it. "I'm not a historian," he says, "and I didn't have much interest in it until folks started publicizing it again about ten years ago [on the fiftieth anniversary of the battle]."

Now his pickup bears a "Screaming Eagles" decal, and he goes to Shenandoah Memorial Park on occasion to pay tribute to fallen heroes and veterans who have preceded him in death. In time, he, too, will lie there.

And, as the days grow short come mid-December, he remembers The Bulge and Bastogne. "The Germans had to have it," he says, "but they didn't get it."

Floyd Owens's War

Many outfits claimed to have relieved the 101ˢᵗ Airborne in Bastogne. I know we did.
—Floyd P. Owens Jr.

A few nights back—and a few days after I had the pleasure of interviewing him—Floyd Owens and Frances, his wife of fifty years, were watching the Hollywood movie *Battle of the Bulge* in their Bayberry Court duplex.

As scenes relative to the infamous "Malmedy Massacre" flickered across the screen, Frances looked over at her husband, who seemed transfixed by the images.

Later, Floyd would tell Frances of a day more than sixty-five years ago when he, a platoon guide in Company B, 320ᵗʰ Infantry Regiment, 35ᵗʰ Infantry Division, saw victims of this massacre, all GIs, still lying in a snow-encrusted Belgian field.

It's fascinating to witness how memories, long buried, can come flooding back, seemingly in an instant. Floyd also recalled a fleeting interaction with English-speaking German soldiers disguised as American MPs, another notable element of "The Bulge" covered well by the motion picture.

But movies, as well we know, are—and can only be—fanciful representations of riveting albeit jarring real-life experiences. Floyd, like so many members of his "greatest generation," fought—many, as he says of himself, by "presidential invitation"—and then, upon doing their duty, came home to raise families and live productive lives.

Floyd, a Jefferson County native, is emblematic of this breed. His medals, which include a Bronze Star, were consigned to a dresser drawer, out of sight for years. They are now proudly displayed in a shadow box.

You see, like so many veterans, only as his days grow shorter—he turns eighty-seven on Thursday—has Floyd deigned to reflect anew on that time when he was, at once, a soldier and young.

We, as the legatees of such sacrifice, are so much the better for these reflections. Even when Floyd, clearly downplaying his contribution to the war effort, says, "A lot of bullets missed me."

The rest of his story? A "certified, bona fide rifleman," Floyd landed in the south of France on D-Day+21. He was a "replacement soldier," which, he says, was "one of the most humiliating experiences one can endure." That is, taking the place of someone either killed or wounded in action.

But a lieutenant named Gus Miller saw something in Floyd and made him, "a lowly PFC [private first class]," a platoon leader. And so, along with the rest of the 35th, a division often thrown in the breach, he raced at the behest of General George Patton to the Christmastime relief of the besieged defenders of Bastogne during The Bulge. He remembers crossing a snow-covered field near the town under withering German fire.

After recovering from wounds sustained weeks later in a mortar attack— "my face was a bloody mess," he says—Floyd earned his Bronze Star "for heroic service near Heberingshof, Germany" on March 8, 1945. He led an attack that cleared Germans from a wooded area, capturing eight enemy soldiers in the process, and then took part in a "successful assault" on a "group of buildings" in the town.

Floyd's war ended two months later on the Elbe River, twenty-three miles short of Berlin, when the decision was made, he says, to let Russian troops capture Germany's capital.

Upon returning home to Charles Town, Floyd started a trucking business, hauling cattle. He also sold cars and opened a Buick dealership in Front Royal. He and Frances married in 1959 and raised two sons.

And through all those years, his medals, like his memories, lay buried. Looking back, Floyd offers an explanation: He didn't "want people to think I was bragging."

And so you have the mindset of a generation—our "greatest."

A Bridge to Victory

I'll tell you, our outfit was outstanding, so many outstanding fellas. We were a good outfit.
—Richard Clark Purcell, 157th Engineer Combat Battalion

Remember that oft-quoted line from the Tom Cruise hit *Jerry Maguire*, "You had me at 'hello'"?

Well, for someone to "have me," as it were, all he or she needs to say is, "I am a World War II veteran." So great is my desire to learn all I can about our "greatest generation."

Thus, when Richard Clark Purcell of Brucetown stopped by the *Star* office in late November, my buddy Bobby Ford knew enough that I would like to chat with the spry and talkative eighty-five-year-old.

Richard Purcell. *Courtesy of the Stewart Bell Jr. Archives, Winchester, Virginia.*

I was out at the time, but when Mr. Purcell returned last week, we settled in for a rather extended stroll down Memory Lane, through France and Germany—and finally Brucetown.

Mr. Purcell's initial reason for coming in was to remind someone—anyone—at the *Star* that the anniversary of the Battle of the Bulge was coming up, and he had a newspaper clipping about General Patton pertinent to that climactic battle that he wanted to share.

I decided on the fly that next week's "Pike" would be devoted to that anniversary and to Mr. Purcell's memories of "Ol' Blood and Guts." But while I had Mr. Purcell in my sights and willing to talk, I wanted to know a little bit about his life and wartime experiences. He was an eager participant.

As I quickly learned, Mr. Purcell has called but two houses home—both in Brucetown and within sight of each other. But when the inevitable call from Uncle Sam came in the spring of '43, he was working in the Baltimore shipyards. On April 28 of that year, he and thirty-nine others from Frederick County—bearing such names as Dove and Dodson, Sirbaugh and Singhass—boarded a bus for the induction center at Camp Lee, southeast of Richmond.

Mr. Purcell, as would seven others from the Winchester area—including Ralph Lamp, for years a city postman after the war—would join the 157th Engineer Combat Battalion. Their next stop: Camp Maxey, Texas.

As Mr. Purcell would explain, the primary tasks of the combat engineers were "taking care of the roads, laying mines and building bridges" for the infantry and tank divisions.

"The biggest thing," he said, "was getting the troops over the bridges." More often than not, this meant erecting, on the spot, the handiwork of Sir Donald Bailey. The "Bailey bridge," a sectional steel span, was one of the wonders of the war. But by the men obliged to build them piece by piece, they've been described as "pure hell."

Mr. Purcell and the 157th landed on Utah Beach in late June 1944, nearly three weeks after D-Day, after spending the better part of six days languishing aboard their transport in the English Channel.

The 157th's first stop, Mr. Purcell said, was the ravaged French town of Volognes, where it helped clear the streets of debris. Then, in early August, it was on to the pivotal crossroads city of St. Lo, still burning from incessant bombardment—all the while striving to keep up with Patton and his fast-moving tanks.

By mid-August, the Allies were closing in on Paris, and two days after the city was liberated, Mr. Purcell and Company C commenced construction of a most memorable Bailey bridge, across the Seine at Mantes Gassicourt near the French capital. The reason Mr. Purcell remembers it so well is because his unit started building the span on August 21, his twenty-first birthday.

He also recalls the incessant aerial attacks, seven in all, that accompanied the arduous work of unloading the components of the bridge and spanning the Seine. Mr. Purcell was gulping down some late-morning C-rations when the first explosions shook the ground. But as he and his mates would later realize, "It was our own guns shooting at the [German] planes."

"You'd get scared at first," he says, "everyone did. But then you'd go normal."

A Prayer at Christmas

The clipping—World War II veteran Richard Clark Purcell's real reason for paying the *Star* (and, ultimately, me) a visit—is yellowed and brittle, befitting its age.

It came from the Saturday, December 29, 1945 edition of the *Baltimore News-Post*, a newspaper long since gone. On its outer margin, just barely legible, are words scrawled in pencil: "I loved this man from the beginning."

Such sentiments are sorta funny, given that Brucetown's Mr. Purcell, now eighty-five and a still-proud vet of the 157th Engineer Combat Battalion, never actually laid eyes on "this man" in question. But, as he says, he and the 157th spent a goodly amount of time trying to keep up with his tanks as they raced through France in the breakout days following D-Day.

Still, Mr. Purcell knew him well—he knew, from often sharing chow with the general's men, that he was hard on his troops and expected a lot of them.

Never was this more evident than sixty-four years ago this Christmas week, when U.S. troops were fighting for their lives—and against the bitter December cold—in and around the besieged Belgian town of Bastogne. For this reason, Mr. Purcell felt latter-day Americans needed to be reminded of General George S. Patton.

Mr. Purcell and his mates were in Alsace when the Germans, in a last-ditch effort to turn the war's tide, drove a deep "bulge" in the Allied lines—

and the call went out for Patton and his 3rd Army. What transpired—what Mr. Purcell wants folks to recall—was one of the more incredible episodes, and feats, in U.S. military annals.

Simply put, Patton—after relieving the 157th, Mr. Purcell says, of "all of our gas"—drove eastward on December 19, 1944, and then turned his entire army on a dime, ninety degrees, in the dead of a most miserable winter to march to the relief of Bastogne, defended by detachments of the elite, and rock-tough, 101st Airborne Division.

Along the way, the oft-profane Patton prayed for better weather, to the point of distributing a Christmas message to his troops, on which was printed this warrior's prayer: "Almighty and most merciful father, we humbly beseech Thee, of Thy great goodness, to restrain these immoderate rains with which we have to contend. Grant us fair weather for battle. Graciously hearken to us as soldiers who call upon Thee that armed with Thy power, we may advance from victory to victory, and crush the oppression and wickedness of our enemies, and establish justice among men and nations. Amen."

The prayer was answered on December 23, as the skies cleared and Allied planes took to the air to bomb German positions and drop much-needed supplies to the men in Bastogne. Patton's tanks arrived three days later, on the morning after Christmas.

Less than five months later, the war in Europe was over. Richard Purcell and the 157th were bound for Salzburg, Austria, on the autobahn, when the welcome news came. Riveted in his memory from that day is the sight of defeated Germans streaming back toward their homeland from Italy.

Mr. Purcell returned home to Brucetown in December 1945. He married his wife of fifty-eight years, Mildred, a war widow with two young children. In time, they had two girls of their own.

Over the years, he split his labors, working in carpentry and construction in the Washington, D.C. area while also tending to his acreage and cattle in northeastern Frederick County.

But, as with many in his generation, that time spent fighting overseas has remained the defining episode of Mr. Purcell's life. He has attended many reunions of the 157th and has even been host to one, held at the Travelodge back in 1991.

In 1995, a year after the fiftieth anniversary of D-Day, he returned to Europe and trod upon the ground he helped liberate. He relished the ten-day experience so much that he flew back the next year and stayed seventeen days.

It is interesting to note that the only bit of terrain Mr. Purcell immediately recognized was that stretch of the autobahn on which he was riding when he learned the war was over—and he'd be heading home.

6

GEORGE CRAIG AT IWO JIMA

A LETTER HOME

Fifty-six years ago this Thursday, a small story appeared on the front page of the *Star*. Its headline read simply, "Local Boy Writes from Iwo Jima." The name of the "boy"? George L. Craig Jr.

Two generations of Handley High students knew Mr. Craig well, first as a biology teacher and then as principal from 1968 to 1985. In March 1945, though, George Craig was a twenty-year-old Marine corporal slogging his way with thousands of other young Leathernecks through the bloody sands and lava rock of that tiny Pacific atoll.

His letter, written from a foxhole ten days earlier, informed his loved ones on North Braddock Street that he was well and, more important, unharmed. Mr. Craig said he had received his first mail from home—including thirty letters from his wife, Jane—since the Marine landing on February 19 and had attended the first church services held on the island.

"This place is a terrible place to be," Mr. Craig wrote, "but I'm glad I'm here instead of the [Japanese]."

Fast-forward fifty-six years: February 19, 2001, found George Craig in the company of former Marines, veterans of Iwo Jima, in Harlingen, Texas, on the campus of the Marine Military Academy (MMA), where a dinner was held in their honor.

Harlingen, located in the Rio Grande Valley, is a special place. Not only is it home of the MMA, a prep school established by Marine veterans, but it is also but a quick hike away from Weslaco, where Harlon Block

George Craig. *Courtesy of the Stewart Bell Jr. Archives, Winchester, Virginia.*

is buried. Block was one of the six men immortalized in the photograph depicting the raising of Old Glory on Iwo's Mount Suribachi. The original plaster cast of the famous Marine Corps monument in Arlington stands on the MMA grounds.

That photo—and a recent bestseller, *Flags of Our Fathers*, penned in tribute to those six men whose deed was captured on film—is the reason for this column. The inspirational book, written by James Bradley, son of one of the flag-raisers, prompted me to ring Mr. Craig, whom I knew to be an Iwo veteran. Two calls to his home on Amherst Street, though, produced nothing but voice-mail messages.

Fortunately for me, Mr. Craig checks those messages. Early last week, he called me at the *Star*—from Texas, where he and Jane have been passing the winter in their motor home. They arrived in the Lone Star State on January 10; how they got there would be the envy of every "travelin' man," even Charles Kuralt.

Since Mr. Craig retired from the city's public schools, he and his wife have spent almost as much time on the road as the late CBS newsman. They have worn out, he says, no less than three motor homes in their travels.

Since leaving Winchester last July, the Craigs have gradually made their way to Mission, Texas, where they have parked their RV. Along the way, they have visited a granddaughter in British Columbia as well as a number of presidential libraries and national parks.

Essentially, they stop where they want to and stay "two days or two weeks," as Mr. Craig says.

Clearly, however, their extended layover in Texas has been extraordinary. Not only did they make new friends among Iwo Jima veterans they had never previously met, but, at the anniversary dinner, they also heard James Bradley speak.

In his speech, Mr. Craig said, Bradley did not address the research that went into his book as much as he did the sacrifices of our "greatest generation"—a generation of "boys" who wrote home from such faraway places as the South Pacific.

Once a Marine...

The Marines are a very elite organization, one of the best fighting units in the world. I just wanted to be part of it.
—George L. Craig Jr.

As George Craig told me last week, there is no such species as "ex-Marines," only "former Marines." "Once a Marine, always a Marine," he said.

Now seventy-six years old, Mr. Craig obviously falls into the "former" category. He is also a graduate—and erstwhile principal—of Handley High. These two distinctions—Marine and Handley alum—are linked, he noted, by that same lifetime distinction: "Once a Judge...."

The "day of infamy" at Pearl Harbor was six months away when Mr. Craig left those hallowed Handley halls as a student in June 1941. When the United States entered World War II, he, like millions of young men of his generation, dutifully registered for the draft. When his call came on April 28, 1943, he decided to enlist in the Marines.

Why the Marines?, I asked, not so much incredulously but with equal parts fascination and awe. I had just finished reading James Bradley's compelling account of the Marines on Iwo Jima, *Flags of Our Fathers*, so I naturally wondered what prompted Mr. Craig's enlistment.

"Patriotism was running at such a fever pitch then," he said.

Actually, as Mr. Craig informed me a few moments later, there was a little more to it than that. As the time neared for him to report to Richmond for his physical, he discussed his enlistment plans with his parents; they were, he said, "none too crazy about it." After all, he was but eighteen years old.

However, when he got to Richmond and was faced with the decision of either selecting a branch of service or being drafted into the army, he went with his initial choice. He would become a Marine.

At that time, enlistees could either sign up for a standard four-year hitch or serve at the "convenience of the government," or "COG." Mr. Craig opted for the latter, which meant he would be a Marine for the duration of hostilities, plus an additional six months. He ended up serving a month and two days shy of three years.

After casting his lot with "COG," Mr. Craig went to Parris Island, South Carolina, for boot camp and then to Quantico for artillery school. Rising to the rank of corporal, he was assigned to the 13th Regiment, 5th Marine Division, and made his way to Camp Pendleton, California.

As Bradley points out in *Flags of Our Fathers*, it was at Camp Pendleton that training began for a large-scale attack somewhere in the Pacific. From there, the Marines of the 4th and 5th Divisions embarked for the "Big Island" of Hawaii, where the training intensified.

Christmas Eve and Christmas 1944 found George Craig hauling ammunition onto ships. Shortly thereafter, he and his fellow artillerists loaded themselves onto transports and set sail for the South Pacific. Next stop: Iwo Jima.

FIGHTING WITH WOLVES

The Marines were now being required to perform in a way almost beyond human endurance, both physically and psychologically....
No troops with less esprit de corps than these Marines could have kept going.
—*Marine Corpsman Richard Wheeler,* Flags of Our Fathers

Fifty-six years after storming the beaches of Iwo Jima, former Marine George L. Craig Jr. of Winchester still remembers the nights on that tiny Pacific island as being "the worst."

The Marines were fighting an unseen enemy. The Japanese defenders of Iwo had erected an elaborate system of pillboxes, blockhouses and subterranean tunnels and caves from which to torment the invading Americans.

"We didn't see them, but we just kept hammering away," Craig explained during a recent telephone conversation. "They even dragged their dead back into the caves." But the Japanese did come out at night—and for the famished, sleep-deprived Marines, the "prowling wolves" of General Tadamichi Kuribayashi were the cause of unfathomable "mental and physical anguish."

"The nights were horrendous," Craig recalled. "We had two men to a foxhole, one trying to grab a few winks and the other standing guard."

In the early stages of the campaign, Craig, an artillerist assigned to the 13th Regiment, 5th Marine Division, helped provide howitzer support for the rifle companies of the 27th Regiment. But as the grinding battle wore on, he and his artillery mates were asked to pick up their rifles and report to the front lines as replacements for the battle-weary infantry units.

Though Craig did not engage in any hand-to-hand combat as a replacement—"for which I was very thankful," he says—he did witness the stealthy maneuvering of the Japanese around their "elaborate" fortifications.

His brother-in-law, Private First Class David A. Stewart, was not quite as lucky. Early in the battle, Stewart suffered two bayonet wounds at the hands of a "prowling wolf." The wounds, fortunately, did not prove fatal.

Iwo Jima was originally envisioned as a four-day operation. Instead, it took four days simply to seize the island's highest point, Mount Suribachi, and twenty-five days to declare the island secure.

For some perspective, consider this: The 5th Division left for Iwo Jima on twenty-two crowded transports; its survivors steamed away from the island aboard eight. One-third of all Marine deaths in the forty-three months of America's involvement in World War II occurred in that single battle.

"We were just doing our job," Craig said in retrospect. "When you're that young [he was twenty at the time], you're all confidence; you feel invincible.

"Still, it was a group thing, not individual. Hours of training led to a melding of the troops—and of an esprit de corps unmatched by anyone."

Now seventy-six years old, Craig, former principal of Handley High, worries that the sacrifices made on that bloody atoll—and through all of World War II—"will be relegated to one page in some history book."

"We will try to keep the memory alive," he said.

May he rest assured that as long as America remains free and men and women are still moved by tales of undaunted courage and simple bravery, the gallant men of Iwo will never be forgotten.

7

FOUR FOR VETERANS DAY

In the days and months since I wrote my Memorial Day feature on Winchester's "Mr. Veteran"—the late Bill Butler—and his exploits during the Battle of the Bulge, I've received a number of letters and/or scrapbooks from other World War II vets or their kin.

I would clearly relish giving all these folks "the Bill Butler treatment," but, alas, time and space limitations restrict me from doing so. What's more, as opinion editor of this newspaper, an engrossing daily endeavor, I have but infrequent bites at the feature apple.

Fortunately, I do have this weekly column, which, on this Veterans Day, affords me ample opportunity to tell the stories of these vets, albeit in abbreviated form. The four men profiled are—or were—well-known personages in this community. Many readers, though, may not realize the depth of their wartime service.

Without further ado, allow me to introduce you to four men who were soldiers once—and young.

Edward L. Christianson
Known to legions of local Catholics as "Deacon Ed," the Wisconsin-bred Mr. Christianson went through specialized basic training as a combat medic. Assigned to the 422nd Regiment, 106th Infantry Division, he was transferred to the division's 331st Medical Battalion.

In the opening hours of the Battle of the Bulge, Mr. Christianson, a newly minted ambulance driver, transported wounded from the front to a clearing station. On one such run, he drove his ambulance straight into "the middle of the shooting war." Despite a flat tire and blown radiator, he managed to remove a seriously wounded cavalry sergeant without incident.

A fateful twist: The 106th sustained more than seven thousand casualties in the first three days of The Bulge, many from his old unit, the 422nd. There but for the grace of the God he continues to serve would have gone "Deacon Ed."

WILLIAM H. LOUTHAN

A letter from Mr. Louthan's son Tom, a Winchester attorney, says it all: "While many of our local men gave the supreme sacrifice, I know of no other local veteran who lost an arm at the age of twenty-one."

A "replacement" soldier in the 2nd Armored Division, Bill Louthan landed on Omaha Beach eight days after D-Day. He eventually became a gunner on an M-8 armored car. While on a reconnaissance mission later that summer, he was struck by shrapnel, causing him to lose an arm when a German shell landed near his car.

An insurance agent for forty years after returning to Winchester, Mr. Louthan retired in 1989.

JAMES DOUGLAS BUTLER SR.

Doug Butler and his older brother Bobby were drafted in early 1943. Doug ended up in the 15th Air Force, Bobby in the 8th. Both flew on B-24s.

A nose-turret gunner, Doug says he and his nine-man crew led a "charmed life"—thirty-five bombing missions without a casualty. Bobby was not so fortunate. On a bombing mission over Mainz, Germany, his plane went down and he and his crew with it.

DUANE W. HOCKMAN

A driver in a tank destroyer battalion attached to the 45th Infantry Division, Mr. Hockman saw extensive action—in the final days of the North African campaign, then in Italy at Anzio and during the capture of Rome and, finally, in southern France, where he saw his tank destroyed from under him.

Left: Bill Louthan. *Courtesy of the Stewart Bell Jr. Archives, Winchester, Virginia.*

Below: Doug Butler (*third from left*) poses with crew members of his B-24. *Courtesy of the Stewart Bell Jr. Archives, Winchester, Virginia.*

Captured by the Germans on September 1, 1944, he endured a forced seventy-mile march from Lyon, France, to the German border. He contracted malaria and then pneumonia while imprisoned in Stalag 7A.

A truck driver and then a partner (with son Michael) in a local ambulance service, Mr. Hockman died on February 11 of this year. In October, his widow, Martha, learned he had been named a "Chevalier" in the French Legion of Honor.

This brings me back to Bill Butler. He, too, earlier this year, was accorded the same distinction.

8

"THE MAJOR OF ST. LO"

Howie's Immortality

OK, I'll admit it. When I got into the car Tuesday morning, a typically glorious Fourth of July, I had precious little idea what path this column would take. But driving, even that short trip from Stephens City to Winchester, is good for me. I do my best thinking behind the wheel.

And so this column came together in that tidy fifteen minutes, courtesy of Bill Bennett's *Morning in America* radio show, Toni O'Connor and her musical meanderings and my own fascination with D-Day and Normandy.

How did these three rather diverse entities—lines of thought, actually—conspire to make a column? Here's how:

Bennett's Tuesday program was dedicated to love of country and soldierly sacrifice. This got me to thinking, naturally, about that "longest day" on the Normandy beachheads, which neatly segued into Toni's plans for us next summer—a trip to England with a bunch of her Musica Viva buddies, who are slated to sing in a number of British cathedrals, including Canterbury.

Following this musical grand tour, Toni and I are hoping to skip over the Channel to France to satisfy a long-held dream of mine to visit the D-Day sites.

As I moseyed to the office, my mind started to wander toward that hallowed ground in Normandy—and the exploits of the men who liberated it. One of my favorite stories—so fitting for the Fourth of July—centers on the former German stronghold of St. Lo and a man named Tom Howie.

Major Thomas Dry Howie, a native of South Carolina and a graduate of The Citadel, was teaching English and coaching football at Staunton Military Academy, ninety miles from here, when World War II broke out. He was also an officer in the Virginia National Guard.

In the early-morning hours of June 6, 1944, Howie hit Omaha Beach with the rest of the 116th Regiment, 29th Infantry Division (which also included future Winchester mayor Miff Clowe and the local boys of Company I). Five weeks and a lifetime later, he was given command of the regiment's 3rd Battalion, advancing toward St. Lo.

On July 16, using grenades and bayonets, Howie and the 3rd Battalion cut through the German lines to relieve the isolated 2nd Battalion, suffering from a lack of food and ammunition. Judging the 2nd "too cut up" to continue, Howie pressed forward with the 3rd. On the morning of July 17, he called his commanding officer, Major General Charles Gerhardt, and uttered words well known in World War II lore: "See you in St. Lo."

Shortly thereafter, Howie sustained fatal wounds in a mortar attack. The next day, his soldiers expelled the German defenders and set the stage for a stirring moment.

At Gerhardt's request, a jeep bearing Howie's body on its hood led the victorious column into town. In death, Tom Howie was the first American to enter St. Lo. His body, draped in the Stars and Stripes, was gently placed in the rubble that was once St. Croix Church.

As the story goes, a photographer from *Life* magazine captured the scene. But when the shot was published, army censors had requested that Howie's name not be divulged. He was identified only as "The Major of St. Lo."

Today, Major Howie rests with more than nine thousand of his comrades at the American Cemetery on the bluffs overlooking Omaha Beach. And a bronze bust wrought in his memory graces a traffic circle near the middle of the rebuilt city of St. Lo.

Next summer, I hope to be taking his picture.

Daughter Knows, Cherishes Father's Place

Sally Howie McDivitt was but a child of three when her father marched off to war in 1941, never to return.

She has her dad's memorabilia—the yellowed newspaper clippings and the photos, too. A particular favorite shows him as a cadet at The Citadel, the military college in Charleston, South Carolina.

But memories? Not too many.

McDivitt can recall sitting with her father in his favorite chair, chatting and singing songs. Trips with him to the post at Staunton Military Academy come back to her, as do visions of camping "down on the river" between Staunton and Harrisonburg.

"It's a little bit here, a little bit there," McDivitt says, seated in her spacious Culpeper home. "But of day-to-day life, interactions and conversations, I have little memory."

And truth be told, she adds, "I didn't miss him the way you traditionally define it."

After all, life was good growing up in the bosom of family in Staunton, her mother's hometown. McDivitt would go to college—Converse, then Duke and finally Mary Washington—and earn her degree. She would marry, have four children and then embark on a successful career in the real estate business.

Only then, as an adult, would McDivitt absorb the enormity of her father's place in America's military pantheon. "It's gratifying," she says, "to know that, if I had to lose a parent, I would lose someone like that."

That "someone" is Major Thomas Howie, hero of the battle for the pivotal French crossroads town of St. Lo and, reputedly, the inspiration for Captain John Miller, the Tom Hanks character in the blockbuster World War II movie *Saving Private Ryan*.

Howie, commander of the 3rd Battalion, 116th Regiment, 29th Infantry Division, is mentioned specifically in the resolution honoring the "Blue and Gray" 29th now working its way through the Virginia General Assembly.

"It's hard to believe," McDivitt continues, "that I was fortunate enough to have that kind of parent. Sometimes, I do wonder what my life would have been like had he not died."

And then it hits her: She would have watched him grow old. So to Sally McDivitt, the "Major of St. Lo" will always be in his mid-thirties—and "larger than life."

Thomas Dry Howie was a son of the South—and of South Carolina, where in the "charming little town" of Abbeville he was born. Though slender in stature, at five feet, eight inches and 140 pounds, he excelled on the gridiron at The Citadel.

"He was very well disciplined," McDivitt says. "If he wanted to do something, he kept at it until he did it."

Upon graduating in 1929, he moved north to teach English and French and coach football and boxing at Staunton Military Academy. And he married the former Elizabeth Payne.

Left: Major Thomas Howie's resting place after the Battle of St. Lo, the rubble of the Church of St. Croix. *Courtesy of the O'Connor family.*

Right: Major Howie's final resting place: American Cemetery, Colleville-sur-Mer, Normandy, France. *Courtesy of the O'Connor family.*

Howie also joined the local National Guard unit, and in 1941, when it was activated, he left home and hearth and baby daughter.

On June 6, 1944, Howie hit Omaha Beach, McDivitt says, in the first wave. Surviving that crucible, he rose in the ranks to Third Battalion commander as the 116th was slogging its way toward St. Lo.

By July 17, the battalion—battered, bruised and barely at half strength—had moved within striking distance of the critical town. Divisional commander General Charles Gerhardt ordered Howie forward. Howie replied, "Will do," and then, after giving his officers their instructions, smiled and said, "See you in St. Lo."

Moments later, a German mortar barrage zeroed in on Howie's position. A jagged piece of shrapnel struck him in the back. He uttered, "My God, I'm hit" and died minutes later.

On July 18, the 29th breached the defenses of St. Lo. Gerhardt ordered Howie's body placed on the hood of a jeep to lead the victorious Americans into the town. And there in the middle of St. Lo, amid the rubble of what had once been the Church of St. Croix, his flag-draped body lay in state, a symbol of ultimate sacrifice.

A photographer captured the moment, and *Life* magazine picked up the photo. The remains, in time adorned with flowers, were identified merely as "The Major of St. Lo."

The words "See you in St. Lo" now hold special meaning for Sally McDivitt. She has been to the French city her father helped liberate on three occasions—the last time in 2008, when St. Lo, now a sister city of Roanoke, commemorated the 100th anniversary of Howie's birth.

McDivitt walks the streets, she says, as a "celebrity." Big banners greet her, and even teenagers "come up and want their photo taken with me."

It is proof positive that, more than six decades after the fact, that special part of France still remembers and still honors the memory of men who came in ships or dropped out of the night sky to save it.

Still, the next time she returns—and there will be a next time, she says, now that she's retired—McDivitt will eschew "all the fanfare" in favor of quiet time, so much the better to "contemplate" the true meaning of all that her father and his comrades achieved.

Monument to Major Howie at traffic circle, St. Lo, France. *Courtesy of the O'Connor family.*

She understands fully why Gerhardt issued his famous order, why her father, even in death, led the army into St. Lo. It was about him, and yet it wasn't all about him. "It was specific to him in some respects," she says. "It was not picking someone out of the blue.

"But General Gerhardt wanted that particular accomplishment to be remembered. That's why he ordered the body taken in ahead of the unit—as a symbol of all that went into that campaign."

Either way, as symbol or flesh-and-blood hero, the "Major of St. Lo" still lives.

"THE DUTY OF MEMORY" STILL ALIVE AT ST. LO

The duty of memory—Jean [Mignon] makes sure it is passed on.
They feel very strongly about this.
—Michael Yannaghas, June 14, 2011

It's one of those ironies—and oddities, perhaps—of armed conflict that this phoenix of a city in Normandy, 95 percent destroyed during the Second World War, so proudly and warmly welcomes the latter-day countrymen of those responsible for its destruction.

Ironic, too, is that the fighting man widely revered in this city—an American officer from Staunton—never actually set foot within its confines but fell victim to shrapnel just outside its boundaries one mid-July morning in 1944.

But, as Toni and I and ten fellow sojourners learned firsthand two weeks ago, memory still runs deep in St. Lo and the rest of Normandy. And so, too, does the duty to remember.

On that Tuesday—Flag Day, appropriately, back home—we took time out from tracking the path of Easy Company, 506th Parachute Infantry Regiment, 101st Airborne (the "Band of Brothers" of HBO fame) to honor "The Major of St. Lo," Thomas Dry Howie of Virginia's own 116th Infantry.

For one member of our entourage, former Winchester mayor Larry Omps, the side trip had special meaning. As a cadet at Staunton Military Academy back in the '60s, Larry was a member of the Howie Rifles, named in honor of the English instructor and football coach at SMA who died leading the 116th's 3rd Battalion toward the embattled French city.

I told the story of Howie a few years back in this space, so I'll spare many of the details. Suffice it to say, though, he became the symbol of the savage fight for this city when his flag-draped remains, laid atop the hood of a jeep, led the victorious American column into St. Lo and then were displayed atop the rubble of the Church of St. Croix.

A famous photograph that appeared in *Life* magazine identified Howie merely as "The Major of St. Lo." And his final words to General Charles Gerhardt, commander of the 116th, before a mortar shell took his life—"See you in St. Lo"—have echoed down through the decades.

As Howie's only child, Sally McDivitt, told me last year, her dad's name still resonates among the Norman populace. And this we discovered for ourselves when we ventured to the traffic circle honoring the major in a wreath-laying ceremony.

There to greet us were not only two local historians (and cultural outreach representatives)—Jean Mignon, who as a fourteen-year-old lived through the storm and strife of '44, and Michael Yassaghas—but the city's deputy mayor, Ugo Paris, as well. A reporter also came, notepad and camera in hand, to chronicle the event for the city's newspaper.

Speaking through an interpreter (Mr. Yassaghas), Mr. Paris informed us that the centuries-old Chapel of St. Madeleine, a short walk from where Howie fell, is "not a war museum, but a place of memory for all those who gave their lives for liberation, especially those who traveled thousands of miles."

Larry then laid the wreath beneath the bust of Howie at the traffic circle and, speaking from the heart, said how this simple ceremony "completes a segment of my life"—a Howie Rifleman bearing solemn witness to his unit's heroic namesake.

A tour of the chapel and of the protective tunnels hacked into the rock beneath the city's medieval walls conducted by Messrs. Mignon and Yassaghas followed. During this tour, I posed this question to both men: Why do the townspeople, after all these years, continue to go "the extra mile" for those in any way connected to Thomas Dry Howie?

In halting English, Mr. Mignon said, "It is for what Major Howie did for St. Lo."

They see not the destruction wrought by Allied artillery. They see only him—a man who gave his life not just for "the liberation" but also for them. And so they dutifully remember—always.

ABOUT THE AUTHOR

A native of Jersey City, New Jersey, Adrian O'Connor belatedly followed the advice of his dear mother—"Go to newspapers, young man"—and ended up spending forty years in the inky-wretch(ed) industry. First, though, there were extended pursuits of the history muse, as witnessed by his two degrees in that discipline: BA, Randolph-Macon College (1976) and MA, University of North Carolina–Chapel Hill (1979). A sportswriter by original desire, O'Connor chased all sorts of bouncing balls for a decade before turning to opinion writing mixed with dabbling in features and columns. Over those forty years, his ports of journalistic call included Petersburg, Emporia, South Boston, Danville and Winchester, all in Virginia.

This book is O'Connor's second compilation of writings for The History Press. He resides in Stephens City, Virginia, in a rambling old Victorian pile with his wife, Toni, and two black cats, the curmudgeonly Eli and the coquettish Licorice.